Feng Shui *for*
Children's Spaces

Feng Shui *for* Children's Spaces

A Parent's Guide to Designing Environments in Which Children Will Thrive

Nancilee Wydra

CB

CONTEMPORARY BOOKS

Library of Congress Cataloging-in-Publication Data

Wydra, Nancilee.
    Feng shui for children's spaces : a parent's guide to designing environments
in which children will thrive / Nancilee Wydra.
        p.   cm.
    Includes bibliographical references (p.) and index.
    ISBN 0-8092-2480-1
    1. Feng-shui.   2. Children's rooms—Miscellanea.   I. Title.
BF1779.F4 W93   2001
133.3'337—dc21
                                                   00-34553

Material on pages 145–146 adapted from Gabriel Mojay, *Aromatherapy for Healing the Spirit*, copyright 1996 by Gaia Books. Adapted by permission of Gaia Books.

Cover design by Kim Bartko
Interior design by Rattray Design
Cover and interior illustrations by Ginny Piech Street

Published by Contemporary Books
A division of NTC/Contemporary Publishing Group, Inc.
4255 West Touhy Avenue, Lincolnwood (Chicago), Illinois 60712-1975 U.S.A.
Copyright © 2001 by Nancilee Wydra
Printed in the United States of America
International Standard Book Number: 0-8092-2480-1
01 02 03 04 05 06 VL 18 17 16 15 14 13 12 11 10 9 8 7 6 5 4 3 2 1

To my son, Zachary Abraham Wydra, who gave me far more
love, encouragement, and laughter than a parent dare hope
for. And to those other children in my life, whom I cherish:

> Chad Breitenfeld
> Chloe Root
> Barnaby Root
> Rebecca Street
> Tommy Street
> Matt and Alex Greene
> Patrick Huot
> Shanna Amsler
> Lenny Bourla-Yanor
> Baby Kroll

I salute you with all my love.

And to Dr. Anita Rui Olds's class at Harvard's Child Care
Institute—I learned much from her and her students, especially
Sue Norman whose help was inspirational in creating this book.

Contents

Introduction

LIFE IS MOTION. From the instant the sperm and egg unite, the process of movement and change never abates. Perpetual movement and change are universal. I am not a scientist, but I am interested in thinking about the nature of our universe. I ponder the possibilities of how our way of thinking could be mistaken, limited, and misguided. The Greek philosopher Aristotle (384–322 BC) defined the earth as the center of the universe. At that time, perhaps for mystical reasons, it was hard for humans to grasp that our own planet might be orbiting around another mass that is static in neither quantity nor position. Physicists, such as Stephen Hawking, author of *Black Hole and Baby Universes*, speculate that our universe is an infinite curved space in which there is no beginning or possibly no end and that time, as we believe it to be, doesn't exist. What, you may be thinking, does this have to do with children?

As it turns out, it has a great deal to do with children, because in this book I attempt to view how an environment can be shaped for children in fresh ways. The nature of *truth* constantly shifts, and those who can grasp the new will reach heights formerly unscaled. Unburdening us from the mundane or the limits of ready-made furnishings, I hope to help uncover possibilities in your home heretofore unconsidered. Place should help stretch a child's possibilities. An environment must support a child's self-actualization within the context of his or her imagination. The content of the physical world can be a useful tool for shaping what each child seeks and fully exploring the possibilities surrounding life.

An Environment's Essential Job

Before I can share my ideas with you, we must be in agreement on certain principles of this book. It is essential that you, the reader, understand how important a role the environment plays when creating a child's habitat. Only then can you begin to use this book to build a successful, unimpeded framework in your home for the ultimate well-being of your growing child.

An environment should offer children enough options so that they can find their own worth and center. It should provide enough structure to support physiological safety, provide enough redundancy and cohesion to support an emotional sanctuary, be complex enough to challenge, and be easy enough to manipulate to expedite and advance mastery.

It is not by simplifying elements or assigning specific functions that a space offers a dynamic experience. A space must include enough multidimensional opportunities so that it forms a springboard for all experience. Providing the optimum condition for only one activity can further that single activity but not the ancillary opportunities that every experience potentially affords. When a child picks up a stick, that stick has the possibility of being imagined as anything from an orchestra conductor's baton to a space probe's atmospheric detector. In the same way, a blank piece of paper urges a child to delve into his or her own imagination—more than would the outlines in a coloring book. The less structure infused in each setting, the broader the results may be. Within the context of less structure there should be opportunity for extremes. An environment should be both formal and flexible to afford concrete as well as conceptual experiences. A child's environment must be rich with complex factors yet sparse enough for the imagination to spill over onto its surface.

Young children wonder out loud why the sky is blue and what happened to Grandpa's hair. Older children ask questions of enormous complexity, such as If we can know the past, then why not the future and how does light travel, anyway? Seeing the unresolved is childhood's special field of scrutiny. Only when children learn about absolutes does it become harder for them to notice the unseen. The more we instruct children in the preferred and fixed ways of being, the more obstacles we place in the way of their intrinsic propensity for inquiry.

An environment must function like a breath of air. While it is a specific combination of forms, it has the advantage of being formless, unencumbering, and pervasive. Like the act of breathing, an environment should give children what they need and expel what is not necessary or desirable. To model an environment after the function of breath is to understand that the content of the physical world transmutes into a child's soul through osmosis. As if by inhaling, what is out there becomes what is inside.

⊚　　　⊚　　　⊚

While each child has distinct and unique potential, the tiny flame lodged inside each child can come to full brilliance only when an atmosphere that nurtures surrounds it. To help you grow a space that offers options, envelops with safety, inspires the range of human emotions, and endorses unfolding is the spirit of this book. It is with a great deal of joy that I offer a small contribution to the lives of your children.

To the children in all of us and the children who will become us, my love and ideas,

Nancilee Wydra

Feng Shui *for* Children's Spaces

PART I

The Basics

1

The Value of Feng Shui in Shaping Children's Spaces

E xploring reality is an ongoing process of childhood, and a child's investigation is shaped by the content of the physical world. (By *content* I mean all of the furnishings, artwork, fabrics, and any other items used for decorative or utilitarian purposes in a room.) The objects that fascinate children are typically everyday items, for children construct, shape, and fashion whatever is available into situations, scenarios, and landscapes that excite, express, and transmute *what is* into *whatever*. Feng shui looks closely at all of the things we surround ourselves with in our homes and how they affect us. In other words, feng shui reveals how colors, shapes, textures, smells, tastes, and sounds surrounding us affect our emotions, imagination, and enmeshment with ourselves and others. The physical world constructs a three-dimensional reality. The magic is that everything provides us possibilities to help a child develop his or her spirit, mind, and body to its highest potential.

Children select and use anything available, not just what is specifically procured for them. Understanding of how to select patterns of fabrics, wall colors or furnishings, placement and shape of furniture and accessories throughout a home can assist in positively reinforcing messages that are consistent with a child's needs. What children can see and touch, move or enfold becomes an ongoing forum for learning about life. When shaping your child's environment, be cognizant of the fact that all of his or her senses are ripe to be stimulated and enthralled. Since all activities are contained within a physical space, your learning about how that space affects development seems not just reasonable but essential.

While a great deal of research is performed to investigate how primary caretakers exert influence on a child's evolving personality, not enough attention is paid to how the physical environment impacts a child's development. The principles of feng shui reveal the importance of how an early environment can constrain or expand a child's competence and eventually can even shape the way he or she approaches many life situations. While this book will illuminate some general principles of feng shui, it aims to show how to construct an environment that will support those qualities you wish to foster in a child and those a child's innate persona wants to express.

While ancient feng shui does not specifically acknowledge life cycles, it acknowledges common human biological reactions. Feng shui informs us that humans have common reactions because of shared biology. For example, the eye is a mechanism that translates light and movement. Therefore, the amount of light and motion in any environment can make a huge difference in how vividly the space is experienced. A child may be distracted from playing if a TV is on, flashing colors and making sounds, which makes it hard for the child to focus.

What Distracts the Eye

what is outside a window
a television
other children moving
    around a space
an open door
a singularly bright lamp

a painting with sharply contrast-
    ing colors
a mobile
a clock or a mechanism with
    moving parts

The eye sees light first and movement second. To capture children's attention or assist them in focusing, be sure they are not facing a window or a moving object.

Symbols

The environment confronts us with a series of symbols. Some are universal, such as shape and color, and some are culturally learned (such as an upturned light switch means the light should be on). Symbols work as automatic buttons that animate a response and then channel it. A *symbol* can be defined as "an image that releases and directs energy." For example, when we see the color red in any context, we automatically respond with excitement, a quickening of breath, and a sharpening of intellectual and mental activity. However, if the object's form is more significant than the color, then the form takes precedence over the color. For example, in the case of, say, giving an infant a red bottle filled with milk; the food (form) is more important than the red (color).

Here's another example. Suppose you go out and purchase a red comforter to perfectly match the color of the décor of the nursery, with the thought that a down-filled cover will be soft, warm, and comforting and enable your child to feel good before going to sleep. As you read this book you will learn that red sparks enthusiasm and energy. You now recognize that the comforter's color does not match how you want your child to feel prior to going to sleep. You may even discover that with this new purchase your child's bedtime pattern changes: your normally content child becomes cranky and irritable instead of drifting off to sleep peacefully. The culprit in this case could be the color red.

When used inappropriately, universal symbols may deliver messages that are antithetical to the desired behavior. Here's a list of some common items on which inappropriate choices of color deliver a confusing message.

Chapter 7 explains in detail why these colors may not be suited for the items.

ITEM	COLOR'S MESSAGE	DESIRED MESSAGE
Red comforter	Stimulation	Provide security
Blue game table	Self-absorbtion	Interact with others
Green rocking chair	Change in motion	Be soothed and relaxed
White nooks	Exposes and shows off	A place to be sheltered
Black flooring	Depth with no end	A springboard on which to fly or reside
Orange desk	Need to be with others	A place to focus and concentrate
Purple plates	Honor the internal process	Learning sociability
Yellow bedsheets	Clarity and illumination	Relax and let go

Innate and Imprinted Symbols

Once you can recognize that many symbol systems are practically universal, you may begin to wonder, do the symbols then appear innately in the psyche, or are they imprinted, or both? The answer is both. You then might wonder, What is the difference between the intrinsic version and the imprinted one? The difference between the two is important to understand.

First, let's consider an **innate symbol**. Imagine a newly hatched chicken seeing a hawk fly overhead. Consider the phenomenon that the chick will, without prior experience, dart for cover. If a robin or a sparrow were to fly overhead, the baby chick would not respond. But somewhere in chicken brains there is stamped a shape of a hawk that evokes sheer terror. In fact, scientists have made wooden models that imitate the form of a hawk. When such models are drawn across the coop on a wire, the chicks run for shelter. Yet, if the same model is drawn across backwards, *the chicks do not react*. Therefore, the response is innately embedded in the psyche of all newly hatched chicks; it need not be learned and is not unique to any one chicken. These responses are known as *innate response mechanisms* or *stereotypical responses*.

Do children possess innate response mechanisms? What universal symbols are embedded in all children's brains that cause them to respond to stimuli in the physical world? Some would argue that the generalized fears of spiders, rodents, and snakes are a human's innate response to predators that were as deadly as a tiger but hardly as intimidating. The fact is that the power of symbols within our human species is profound and contributes to inherent responses in all of us unless and until we are taught differently. The beauty of feng shui is that its backbone is the innate response mechanisms common to all.

Imprinting is another phenomenon in which a particular model is fastened to the psyche. You may have seen a baby duckling waddle after its mother. But if the mother duck is absent and a human being is the first living entity that it sees, then the baby duck will follow that person just as if it were the mother duck. The duck's instinct to trail after a mother is innate, but what constitutes the actual mother is not. What is available at first sight is imprinted on the duck's psyche as "mother." Therefore, imprinting has elements of individuation, whereas stereotypical responses do not.

Adult humans experience imprinting in the form of falling in love. At the biologically right time, hormones kick in and the urge to mate and "fall in love" overtakes us. The specifics of falling in love are, in part, learned through the cultural context in which you are reared. However, at the moment of physical and psychological readiness, Mr./Ms. Right or Wrong waltzes into your life and voilà, you are in love. Imprinting occurs when you are ready, but you are imprinted to the one that is available.

Childhood is filled with many more moments of imprinting readiness than in later stages of life. Therefore, what is placed in children's environments has significance in shaping their reactions throughout life. Feng shui's underlying principles of the Tao, yin and yang, and chi provide some basic understanding of the influences of formative experiences. Feng shui speaks to the foundation underneath biology and culture first and then examines the influences of culture and psychology.

In my work over these last twenty-five years of exploring the power an environment exerts on humans, I have developed what I consider a **pyramidal hierarchy** of the imprint of the influences of place, or what I call **pyramid feng shui**. Pyramid feng shui alludes to the many systems supporting the whole. Every completed form is dependent on the successful actualization of its parts. Dissecting the whole to view its parts is the philosophical underpinning of pyramid feng shui.

Lifetime Events
The Individual's Psychology
Culture
Human Biology
Physical Sciences

The influences of place on people

Put simply, this pyramid is built on physical sciences, human biology, culture, the individual's psychology, and lifetime events.

"There is nothing new under the sun" is an accurate statement, for all new forms are based on fundamental patterns. For example, a computer bit acts much like an individual living cell. Cell biologist Bruce Lipton told me that when he began reading his new computer's manual he kept thinking that the information in it had a familiar ring. Grabbing a basic biology book from his shelf, he leafed through to the pages that described a cell in the most fundamental way. There were striking similarities! From that moment in the early 1980s, Lipton has toured the country illuminating audiences about how physical properties rely on patterns that repeat themselves in many forms over and over again. In a nutshell, the world, it seems, is finitely complex, and the secret for understanding the many processes is to grasp the fundamental strategy and see how it repeats itself over and over again.

In feng shui principles, water and the sky are colored blue because blue expresses the inherent nature of these entities. In feng shui we assign personality descriptions to colors, and when we evaluate where in nature these colors are found we discover that the color's description aptly defines the object. For example, yellow is the color that most closely represents the sun and is also the color of the cells in our eyes called the *macula lutea*, which provide visual acuity. In feng shui when we want to create a clear, consistent message that aids concentration and clarity of focus, we use the color yellow. It is not a coincidence that the #2 lead pencil is coated with yellow paint, for in our collective psyche we gravitate to those objects that best support an activity. In another example, nutritionist Adelle Davis pointed out in her book *Let's Have Healthy Children* that children would instinctively eat a balanced diet so long as they had not been trained otherwise. By nature, human beings strive to survive and will, unless pointed in another direction, choose those things that best aid their thriving.

Culture

Culture is a compelling factor, for we are all operating within the confines of what we have learned. Children find the messages of their macro- and microcultures represented in their toys, homes, schools, and media programming as well as the attitudes and messages transmitted to them by their caretakers. Early on, humans are trained to believe that acting in one way is correct and another way is not.

If you have traveled to foreign countries or been in areas of the country very different from your own, you may have experienced mild to startling culture shock.

Winifred Gallagher's book *The Way We Are* is a study of a child whose inherent personality was the key to surviving early emotional and physical traumas. The key to this child's success, it is speculated, was her "starlike" personality qualities. When she was hospitalized at an early age, she charmed the staff so thoroughly that she was emotionally adopted and lavished with more positive attention than the other kids. Winning the hearts of those

I almost didn't survive my travels through India, for I was unaccustomed to and clueless about its culture when I arrived. For one thing, I didn't know that it is impolite to disappoint a person. Rather than telling me, for example, that the train I was asking about left ten minutes ago, those I asked about it would provide less specific information. They would say something like, "Oh yes, that's track number 10," which was interpreted by me as meaning "Go to track 10 to catch the train." Culture teaches us how to act, and yet we are completely unaware of the depth and details of our education. Only when confronted by someone who has not been similarly trained do we get a glimpse of how enmeshed we are with our culture's rules.

around her worked to her advantage in a big way; she survived, even thrived, when the odds were decidedly stacked against it. Gallagher aims to reexamine the nature versus nurture question and provides strong evidence that our own innate personality strongly affects the outcome of our lives.

Finally, no human lives in a vacuum, and the historical time and physical location we are born into affects us in many ways. My parents' experience with the Great Depression of the 1930s skewed their views on financial security. As someone who lived through prosperous times, I did not share their fears of poverty or their desire to stockpile in readiness for potential future disasters. Depression, wars, or other momentous events are one category of events that have an impact on the individual, but equally important are the events that happen to you and your much smaller inner circle of family, friends, and community.

When I was five, I went to art classes. One day a classmate asked which church I would be attending for the upcoming holiday. When I told my classmate that I was Jewish and didn't go to church, I came face to face with my first experience of anti-Semitism. It stunned me. The child accused my ancestors and me of all kinds of atrocities that I hadn't a clue about. So traumatic was this singular early-childhood event that there were times when I was growing up that I didn't admit to being Jewish. Your child may experience a neighbor's home burning down, a car accident, or a deeply hurtful personal affront. We all encounter specific lifetime events that play a role in shaping our lives. The trick is to have more positives than negatives.

Life is shaped day by day, event by event, and parents have the responsibility of being aware of the events taking place in their child's universe and being appropriately responsive. This book will equip you with additional tools to give you the flexibility to be proactive and reactive in shaping a physical environment to support positive imprints created by place.

2

The Tao and Early Childhood's Three Stages

How we are connected to all processes and content in the physical world is the keystone of Tao. *Tao*, the Chinese word for "path," is in the broadest sense the way the universe functions. It is the path taken by natural events, observable phenomena, like day following night effortlessly and water invariably flowing downward to the lowest level. So the very basic meaning of Tao is "the cycle of circumstances and events that manifests a process or entity."

In a sense, children are innately Taoists, for childhood is a constant investigation and acceptance of the ways things are. This investigation progresses in stages of increasing complexity and sophistication. A parent's obligation is to be aware of these stages and provide positive experiences appropriate to each stage.

Nonverbal communication consists of a reductive simplification of the complex symbolic abstractions of language and meaning into pictorial forms. By providing appropriate communication between the content of the physical world and a child's undisclosed imagination, a parent can influence his or her child's developing self-esteem and behavior.

The periods of childhood that this book deals with are as follows:

- the Me, Myself, and I stage (birth to eighteen months)
- the Magician stage (eighteen months to three years)
- the On the Road to Reason stage (three to six years)

These three stages of development are described below generally, but as any parent knows, every child develops uniquely. Specific inclinations, be they formally categorized or not, must be taken into account, and some children will linger in one stage longer while some will seem to catapult past a stage. Specific considerations for accommodating some physical conditions are covered in Chapter 16, "Special Needs."

Me, Myself, and I (Birth to Eighteen Months)

During the first eighteen months of life a child has no real cognition of the world beyond what is directly connected with physical needs. Learning to distinguish self from others is, especially in the first four months of life, a slow, ongoing process. During that period, it appears that an invisible web is spun around the child and the primary caretaker through physical contact, and scent, touch, sound, and sight. Selma Fraiberg, former professor of child psychoanalysis at the University of California School of Medicine, suggests in her groundbreaking book *The Magic Years* that infants receive a great many impressions through being in physical contact with their primary caretakers. These contacts contribute in the forming of the child's image of him- or herself. Because there still is no visual memory, other sensory experiences become the language the world and caretakers speak.

Parents can build a foundation of feelings of safety and protection that will help cushion the child from the shocks of life. This cushioning effect is apparent even during the earliest weeks of a baby's life when digestive discomfort is soothed by being held. Later in life a child who sits on a parent's lap to receive an injection tends to withstand the discomfort better than one standing apart from his or her parent.

In order to build consistent sensory experiences leading to feelings of pleasure, satisfaction, and protection, incorporate consistent scents, sounds, and textures into an infant's environment.

Scent

Infuse the scent worn by you, the primary caretaker, on the baby's bedsheets and clothes. A good method is to buy unscented laundry soap and add your own scent to the water when washing.

You may want to refer to the scent list in Chapter 13 to discover what different scents communicate. After learning about scents you may want to alter your daily scent by switching to soaps, hair conditioners, face creams, and so forth whose scents send a message you wish to communicate. Be sure to use products whose primary ingredient communicates the messages you wish to reinforce. If, let's say, lemon's message of alertness and clarity is desired, then a lemon-based body soap, a lemon detergent, and a lemon-scented cleansing product will consistently reinforce this state of being.

Be sensitive to any allergic reaction a product may elicit. Our modern Western world is permeated with many products containing chemicals that compromise the immune system. Use the real thing instead of a chemical substitute.

Susan Rundle, a Massachusetts feng shui practitioner specializing in children's spaces, relates the story of her son's first year at a sleep-away camp. At home his pillow cover was scented with her perfume, because he had an easier time falling asleep when he was provided an olfactory connection with her. She sent him off to camp with a scent-drenched pillow cover to ease the transition. Not long after, the camp counselor called her, panic-stricken, to say that her son needed another perfumed pillow cover to help him fall asleep at night. Luckily he was only about an hour away, so she was able to saturate another pillow cover and bring it to him.

Rundle tells me she was never concerned about this attachment (actually she felt flattered), and eventually he just naturally grew out of it. Obviously, her son connects strongly with scents, and smell is a comforting way of connecting to those he loves.

Unlike her son, Rundle says her daughter has no particular connection to scent but can't sleep at night unless there is nonmusical sound (almost mimicking the sound of voices) present. Be alert to the differences among siblings, for each child may need different sensory emphasis.

Sound

Sound is our first connection to life outside the womb. A mother's heartbeat, gurgling digestive sounds, and muffled voice are transferred through layers of skin and muscles.

An early psychology textbook that discussed an experiment that looked at the efficacy of surrogate mothers dramatically demonstrated the importance of sound in development. One group of baby monkeys was given a chicken wire shape covered with terry cloth that had a ticking clock lodged inside it. A second group of baby monkeys was given an identical model without the clock. The second group developed at a slower rate than the first group, which was raised with the ticking surrogate.

Sound is an essential nutrient for development. By infusing sound into an infant's room, you will link the baby to a vital source of developmental nutrition. Here are a few items that can add sound to your baby's bedroom:

ticking clock	recorded sounds of nature
metronome	sound-producing mobiles
drum music	bells fastened to doors
classical music	wind chimes

Touch

As with all mammals, humans originally lived in natural surroundings. Our species emerged in tropical climates, and most activities were conducted outdoors in direct tactile contact with nature. Nature provides a multitude of tactile experiences underfoot as well as on other skin surfaces. Intermittent breezes, cool spots in shaded areas, and the penetrating warmth of the sun provide thermal variety in any location. Sitting on dirt feels infinitely different from leaning on a bed of wild grasses. Thus, nature affords us a whole array of subtle, palpable body experiences.

Tactile connections are fundamental in early childhood. Even at the height of summer, some of us feel comfortable sleeping only when wrapped in a blanket. This proclivity most likely originates from feeling secure and warm in utero and as a newborn does when cradled. Since many infants flip off covers or bunch them up because the covers are irritating to them, provide your baby with a weighty, warm object to replicate a blanket's innate comfort. Place a warm water bottle in the crib and cover it with a terry cloth mitten that fits its shape for the infant to cuddle up to. (You can spray the mitten with a scent that adds to the Tao reinforcement.)

Swathing an infant from head to toe cuts down his or her tactile experiences and stimulation. To be provided with a host of different choices of diverse, touchable materials tends to arouse and motivate a young child. When selecting clothing, bed linens, and other materials that come in contact with your child, be sure to include a broad range of diverse textures. Include items that represent the tactile diversity listed below.

soft	rigid
hard	warm
piled fibers	cool
smooth	

The Magician (Eighteen Months to Three Years)

At around eighteen months children begin to understand that they are not the initiator of all activities. They begin to sense that their powers are in fact limited and that the satisfaction of needs is dependent on others.

It is the acquisition of language that teaches the Magician to be lured into this new way of thinking, for who in his or her right mind would give up the feeling of controlling the universe without there being some pretty compelling benefits? It appears language provides that compelling force. Through language the physical world is evaluated and shaped for children in the Magician stage. At the beginning of this stage, single nouns such as *mama*, *dada*, *cookie*, and perhaps the name of the family pet or a stuffed animal are sufficient to communicate. Verbs or more descriptive adjectives and adverbs are still secondary to naming objects.

To further a child's connection to the physical world, create opportunities for exploration of a great diversity of objects, ones that are common and part of everyday life and those that are more uncommon. A drawer or cupboard of baskets filled with such objects can be placed within child's reach in an activity area.

Common Objects

flatware	cups	crayons
pots	books	locks
egg beaters	ticking clocks	pillows
whisks	paper	

Uncommon Objects

kaleidoscope	makeup brushes	wire
springs	dowels, all sizes	mechanical innards
bungee cords	netting	

In the Magician state a child is empowered by an audience. Therefore watchful adults and other children are an attribute while investigating the surroundings.

Also during the stage, fantasy reigns, and the Magician may not play with familiar or even carefully selected toys as frequently as those objects that he or she can convert to the flights of fancy triggered by imagination. It's hard to give up a kingdom. Consider having available objects to connect the Magician with the actual environment yet that can be used in the fantasy world. The items listed below can help the child convert reality into fantasy, a necessity for the child to transcend the Magician stage:

dowels, sticks	mop heads	pillows
tissue paper	area rug	random floor tiles
fabric, all sizes and	wigs	hats
textures	cardboard boxes,	shoes (adult-sized)
large rubber bands	all sizes	colorful clothes
to attach fabric	pots and pans	(adult-sized)
around dowels,	spoons	
dolls, etc.	stool	

No amount of healthy admonishments or discipline can subvert the natural curiosity of children at this stage. Be indulgent as they examine the surrounding landscape. This will allow them to unveil the mysteries of the physical world as well as encourage a fertile imagination.

On the Road to Reason (Three to Six Years)

The distinction between physical and social development is that the **physical** will take place regardless of outside influences. Unless there is a specific biological abnormality or complete lack of human contact, every child will learn to roll over, sit up, crawl, and walk. Having toys and other things in the environment that will encourage natural development can set a pattern of accomplishment in utilizing one's environment. Remember, with or without encouragement, physical development marches on to its own drumbeat so it is best to have a hand in the tune it plays.

On the other hand, **social** development—the evolution of ideals, standards of conduct, and the control of impulses and urges based on acceptability—is acquired. Before the age of three children have no real motivation to be unselfish or master their tempers. Being "good" is learned through the reactions of and incentives of others.

But at around the age of three years, the beginning of the On the Road to Reason stage, self-control set apart from the disapproval or approval of adults is inculcated. An independent consciousness—or a "me-ness"—begins to form at this stage, and children begin to distinguish themselves from others. This is the stage at which children develop what Sigmund Freud (1856–1939) called the *superego*, which absorbs what is taught and expected into the self. Reacting appropriately becomes an intrinsic part of a child's behavior. The superego is, in its most basic description, the ingesting of the wishes of the parent.

For example, a two year old would have no idea that removing a wallet from a visiting aunt's pocketbook is considered stealing. But a year later that same child may check for observers before putting a hand inside the cookie jar.

The Tao at this stage is expressed through the acquisition of social process. How is a child exalted when achieving social standards? What physical manifestations can underscore approval or recognition of the child's leap toward socialization?

A **reward** is a tangible Tao manifestation; a reward connects us to acceptable social behavior. Reward a child with items other than food and toys, such as those listed below.

Tao Considerations for Rewards

stars	trading cards
ribbons	an uncommon outing such as an
flowers	archaeological dig in the back-
a hike	yard or taking a walk to look
a special event	for animal tracks

During the On the Road to Reason stage of development, a very integral process takes place. Children begin to comprehend the uniqueness of their own minds and begin to understand that their minds are a force to be used. The concept of "I know I am me" is taking shape. The awareness of "me-ness" is manifested by children's knowing that others may or may not like to do the same things as they do. The observation of distinguishing characteristics in others is a dramatic stage in human development, for the fundamental knowledge of self is derived from the understanding that the self is separate and distinct.

During this stage children learn about themselves. "How am I different?" "What supports my uniqueness?" Many parents infer these questions and try to satisfy them by allowing their children to select their daily outfits or by purchasing furnishings with their children's input and approval.

During my first year at summer camp, campers housed in my cabin were expected to take turns performing cleanup tasks. After weeks of disappointing enthusiasm for cleanup, our enterprising counselor designed a chart that listed each camper's name, each day, and each cleanup task, plus room for stars. Our counselor stuck a gold star next to each camper's name when she successfully completed the daily assignment. At the end of the week those with seven stars were treated with a small, inexpensive gift.

The counselor was taking advantage of two aspects of social development for American middle-class girls: the desire to excel and the appetite for gifts.

These small steps are a wonderful start to what can be a richer acknowledgment of self.

As children begin shaping the self, they experience the physical environment as an ally, as well as an interpreter of their inner selves. In childhood the self is like a sunken treasure at the ocean floor that suddenly frees itself from the grip of the deep. Everything is new to a child. The first time an item is experienced the impact often unfolds immediately, but sometimes slowly. Many times a child loves something one minute and tosses it aside the next; he or she may be experiencing an unfolding awareness of the object. Just as a cake on a baker's shelf can appear irresistible until it is tasted, at times a child may reject a sought-after object or experience right after testing it. Provide your child opportunities to scrutinize different experiences to increase the likelihood of his or her uncovering an unmanifested interest. Below are three categories of objects that support the exploration of the Tao of content along with examples of each:

Objects that when opened, peeled, or taken apart reveal another aspect
- a peeled orange
- boxes within boxes
- doors, drawers, and fliptops

Objects that hook together, making one part become a section of another part
- paper chains
- beads or Cheerios on a string
- puzzles

Objects that convert from one use to another
- a hand becoming a shadow puppet
- a sheet of paper becoming an airplane
- a spoon becoming a slingshot
- a string forming a cat's cradle

A child emerging from the On the Road to Reason stage is fairly sophisticated and possesses a defined self. Perhaps the hardest thing for parents to do is to separate their own personal knowledge of self from that of their child. The Tao of each child will be different from your Tao and that of other family members. Becoming aware of your own prejudices and proclivities and honoring distinctly divergent traits in your children is an ongoing challenge for parents.

Finally, giving your child an awareness of the diversity of life processes can assist his or her emergence as an empowered self. To support a deepening knowledge of your child's surroundings, provide him or her the most diverse opportunities to discover processes and their consequences. These opportunities will equip your child with the confidence to explore the future.

3

Yin and Yang

The Balancing Act

Variety supplies richness. In nature, places of unending conformity are thought of as extreme and inhospitable to habitation. The barrenness of the Gobi desert with its relentless sun, the severe cold of the earth's Arctic, and the pervasive darkness of unexplored caves are challenges to sheer human survival. A little bit of this and a little bit of that ultimately proves to be better than too much of any one thing for too long. Yin and yang are concepts expressing opposite sides of a similar pole and defining the extremes through which sight, scent, sound, touch, movement, and behavior can be experienced.

All colors, shapes, patterns, sounds, smells, and textures can be gauged on a continuum of yin and yang. Yin experiences are mostly those that induce tranquillity and require or exude little effort. Yang experiences are those that energize us and spurn us to action. If you associate yin with breathing in, a time when you cannot verbalize, for inhaling air precludes speaking, then you will remember that yin provides more internal experiences than does yang. Yang is like breathing out, having the breath to verbalize. Yang experiences are those in which we are likely to express or take action. A typical yin reaction to joy is to get goose bumps, and a yang reaction is to leap in the air and invoke a cheer. Yin and yang represent the extremes of behavior on a continuum of possibilities.

Yin and Yang Experiences

YIN INSPIRES CHILDREN TO BE

Calm	Self-absorbed
Inactive	Motionless
Quiet	Centered
Pensive	Sleepy

YANG INSPIRES CHILDREN TO BE

Excited	Sociable
Energetic	Action-oriented
Talkative	Eager
Involved with others	Alert

Color is a dominant tool for expressing yin and yang in an environment. For example, red is generally a yang color, one that activates and enlivens. Yet, a bright fire engine red is very different from a muted terracotta red. Within red's personality, if you will, fire engine red is yang and terra-cotta is yin in the extent and depth of red's message.

When selecting an appropriate color for furnishing a child's room with paint, bed linens, or furnishings, consider the information in the following table. First look at the general message of each color, and then make the selection between that color's yin and yang qualities.

Every color has the potential to be more yin than yang within the context of its overall message: The brighter the red, the more it excites. Retailers tend to manufacture children's funiture and accessories that lean toward yang colors. Sheets, wallpaper, and furniture made for children are generally easier to find in high-gloss yang colors rather than muted, pale, or deep yin colors. While many children benefit from an energizing yang environment, there are others that are overstimulated by yang colors. Unless it is very obvious that your child is timid, is afraid to socialize, or tends to avoid group activities, it is far better to play it safe by selecting yin colors for his or her bedroom.

While color is a major tool for using yin and yang to shape a physical space, there are other considerations. The list on the following page identifies common household items and features as more yin or yang.

Yin and Yang Personality of Color

COLOR	PERSONALITY	YIN (DARKER OR MUTED)	YANG (BRIGHT AND CLEAR)
Red	Enlivens and activates	Sparks expressing sensitivity toward others	Encourages activity
Yellow	Cultivates clarity and optimism	Helps with focus	Encourages overt examination
Blue	Provides centering and calm	Encourages self-absorption	Imbues pride in self
Green	Encourages learning and change	Guides internal change	Guides learning by doing
Orange	Creates desire to be part of a group	Promotes acceptance of others' choices	Cultivates active desire to be part of a group
Purple	Encourages exploration of unknown	Guides questioning the unusual	Guides acceptance of the unusual
Pink	Provides calm and reduces fears	Soothes emotions	Reduces crying or overt physical reactions
Brown	Stabilizes and radiates safety	Produces a sense of security	Exudes being firmly grounded
White	Activates the expression of self	Encourages mental activity	Encourages seeking answers
Black	Suggests the unknown	Frightens	Invites bravery

Yin and Yang of Common Household Items

TYPICAL YIN CONTENT IN A HOME	TYPICAL YANG CONTENT IN A HOME
Areas of low lighting, such as hallways, and a dining room with a dimmer switch	Areas with bright, overall lighting
A great deal of clutter, which curtails movement	Toys that engage large motor activities
Few furnishings, or spaces that are not complex	Windows without coverings
Window treatments that obscure outside light	Pets, people, and concurrent activities
Silence	Scents of fresh, energizing aromas, such as pine, mint, or lemon
Cool temperatures	Highly polished flooring
Windows or the direction of cool breezes	Lots of choices without clutter
Powerful scents, such as cooking odors	Firm surfaces that provide resistance
Wall-to-wall carpets	Bold, contrasting shapes with large repeating patterns
Plush and padded furnishings	A variety of objects to choose from
Solids, a small repeating pattern, or nonspecific prints	Different sizes of furniture
Emptiness, making for limited choices	Bunk beds
No large or tall pieces of furniture	Glossy painted walls, shiny fabrics, and high-gloss finishes on furniture
Low bed	Intense overhead lighting
No shiny materials or glossy finishes	Lots of windows
Small windows	

Textual Yin and Yang Experiences

YIN	YANG
Fine	Coarse
Wet	Dry
Open weave	Tightly woven
Bendable	Rigid
Nappy	Silky
Smooth	Rough, grainy

Consider a pattern's repeat in terms of yin and yang. Small repeats tend to be yin and large repeats tend to be yang.

In order to balance your child's natural tendencies you may want to adjust the environment to contain more items from the opposite of his or her personality. If your child has any self-esteem issues or seems tentative and shy, you might shape the atmosphere to conform with your child's nature, whether yin or yang. It is not necessary to install all conditions from the tables. Choose judiciously, and when making changes, do so slowly in order observe your child's reactions.

A child's behavior patterns can be encouraged or controlled by his or her environment, and we can shape spaces to be appropriate for the behaviors we want to bolster. When you want to calm a child, use yin. When you want to stimulate a child, use yang. Consider how incorporating yin or yang into the rooms below can influence your family's behavior.

Dining area, where the family shares most meals:
Incorporate yin if you want to control exuberance.
Incorporate yang if you want to encourage conversations.

Main gathering area, the space where the family tends to spend the most time:
Incorporate yin if you want family members to relax and be engrossed in independent projects.
Incorporate yang if you want to encourage conversation and lively activity.

Bedroom, where your child sleeps and/or plays:

Incorporate yin if you want your child to use the room mainly for quiet activities and sleeping.

Incorporate yang if you want to encourage your child to engage in play in his or her room.

You may want to create both yin and yang in one room. For example, one wall of the family gathering space may have a yin area in which rows of books are interspersed with solid, dark accessories and lit by low-wattage spotlights. Another corner of the same room could have a yang area with a highly polished blonde wood game table framed by a colorful poster on the wall and lit by a bright overhead light. Each section's yin or yang feelings would be appropriate for the intended activity. Thus yin and yang can be used in different areas to support the kind of activities a child may become involved with in that location.

The following lists categorize several typical childhood activities as yin or yang. Consider supporting these activities with the appropriate yin or yang atmosphere.

Activities Best Supported by a Yin Atmosphere

coloring	investigating
block building	quiet play
sleeping	listening
reading	napping

Activities Best Supported by a Yang Atmosphere

physical activities	acting
talking games	reacting
playing dress-up	interacting

Use yin and yang as a tool to shape a space to be in accord with your child's needs and proclivities. All content in your home resonates with either yin or yang, and the simple act of moving a picture or camouflaging a color (for example, with an afghan tossed over a chair) can begin the process of making any space more aligned with a child's needs.

4

Chi and the Senses

Chi is Chinese for "life force." In traditional feng shui, chi is often used rather loosely and elusively in describing how good or bad energy moves around a physical space. In pyramid feng shui, we define chi as specifically and experientially as possible. Chi is not elusive; it is how our senses take in experiences from the surroundings. Chi is something seen, heard, felt, or smelled, or the way we move through a space. Therefore when you read in non-pyramid books something like, "the chi goes out the door," it actually means that we feel our visual, auditory, kinesthetic mechanisms being pulled in that direction. "How we take in our physical surroundings" is a more precise way of defining the concept of chi. A chi message is implicit in all furnishings, pictures, toys, or fabric patterns.

The Chi of the Senses

Have you ever walked into a room full of children and instantly experienced the sense of variety among them? Physical form is our immediate perception. Are they girls or boys, tall or short, lithe or sturdy? We notice those in motion first. After sight, the next sense that registers is sound. We notice the children who are speaking, singing, whining, giggling, or laughing sooner than those who are silent. Woven through these initial experiences is scent. In a mere moment, you have a picture of many children's chi.

How we express ourselves is our personal chi, and how we observe others or our surroundings is the way we absorb chi emanating from others. How we take in an object's chi is how we evaluate environmental experiences.

Childhood abounds with nonverbal communication. Therefore it is critical to understand the chi of the senses. Since chi is communicated through the content of the physical environment, it is equally critical to know the messages implicit in it. Freya Jaffke, the Waldolf School expert, writes, "Small children, unprotected, are at the mercy of their immediate environment. Their whole body acts as a single sensory organ unself-consciously uniting external impressions with the child's internal world." Children are sensory alert, taking in the sights, sounds, smells, textures, and opportunities for movement in a single swoop unlike adults, whose past experiences often limit full access to sensory materials. For example, my mother is a master at screening out sounds in part because of her parents' frequent bickering, which was better to ignore than suffer through.

A toy is often more intriguing and used when it satisfies many senses. A child responds to a toy perhaps because it feels soft, can be squished, or emits comfortable sounds. In fact, the more areas of sensory input or chi that a toy incorporates, the more fascinating that object is to a young child. How many pretty toys with nothing but prettiness to offer are left untouched?

Maslow's Hierarchy of Needs

Abraham Maslow, the eminent behavioral physiologist, developed a hierarchy of needs in which he categorizes a physical environment in relation to its importance to humans. Starting from the basic need of survival, he theorizes that the next stage of the human condition cannot be reached until the one below it is fulfilled.

Physiological Needs

Parents must be sure that a child's basic needs are satisfied in a hierarchy of importance in order for that child to focus on a higher level. Physiological integrity is ground zero. Unless a child has the biological capacity for survival, nothing else matters.

Many have had experiences where our physical survival was challenged. It may have been an accident, a disease, or even a high fever. What is striking is that during those moments little else matters. Complete focus is required to overcome, ride out, or mitigate a crisis. Needless to say, physiological integrity is imperative before a human can step up to the next stage. The following conditions create the potential for negative physiological chi:

temperature discomfort
inadequate or detrimental contact with people
high noise level
uncared for bodily functions or physical discomfort

Providing protection from negative chi may be as specific as installing a gate to prevent a toddler from tumbling down a flight of stairs or as non-specific as shielding a baby from such artificial noises as those from TVs, radios, or traffic. In general, think about protecting a child from experiences that are markedly different from what is normally found in a benign natural setting. For example, allergy-causing mold, cold, drafty rooms, or a bone-dry, splintering wood floor are some examples of hazards that can extinguish childhood's normal exuberance. More important information on environmental safety is covered in Chapter 17, "Nontoxic Homes."

In an experiential context, a home contains many potential irritants. To prevent a child's chi from being undermined by physical irritations, be sensitive to how the following affects your child.

Negative Chi and Its Effects

POTENTIAL SOURCE	POTENTIAL EFFECT
Distracting sounds, e.g., television	Distraction from self-involvement
Loud sounds, e.g., vacuum cleaner	Fear
Unending sounds, e.g., washer/dryer, traffic	Tension
Hot to the touch, e.g., stoves, computers, irons	Injury and timidity
Empty spaces	Apprehension for safety
Clutter	Feeling stifled
Self-setting door locks	Becoming trapped
Sharp corners on furniture	Injury

Belonging

Maslow's hierarchy continues with belonging as the next need. One might argue that a young infant is not cognizant of structures supporting social groups. But parents are well aware of children's hesitation toward unknowns. A familiar example is the reaction of a young child to strangers. The sudden appearance of a beard or eyeglasses on a grown-up's face for the first time is benign to an older child, but some infants' instinctive reactions are a tightening of the muscles of their entire bodies and a howl. Later in life we usually temper an overt reaction to strangers or strange things. But the point is, it is common to be fearful of the unfamiliar. How we choose to introduce new materials and how we integrate children into new situations has a great deal to do with how well they embrace new situations throughout life and have a sense of belonging.

The concept of belonging entails being understood. If you have ever traveled to a foreign country and tried to make known your wishes, then you have encountered what preverbal children experience all the time. Without common ground it is impossible to make subtle needs known. Just as a hand gesture (say, of putting food into the mouth) can bridge a language gap among adults, so can parents' use of repetitive sounds to soothe the language gap between babies and adults. To build on that, if singing a song calms a sleepless infant, then playing tranquil music can calm him or her in other situations.

Letting your child experience feelings of being unheard, being ignored, or simply being out of the loop is what you as a parent must guard against. To foster your child's feeling of belonging, keep in mind the considerations in the following list.

Considerations for the Chi of Belonging

Make sure he or she is

integral in social gatherings, by having a child-sized chair, rocker, or blanket centrally located, rather than on the periphery

feeling understood, by exhibiting his or her possessions and expressions in prominent places in your home

having his or her physical needs met luxuriously, with a special blanket, favorite music, preferred foods, and toys or play objects in central areas

> *I remember when I was growing up my parents would set up a children's table at family gatherings. By sequestering the children in a remote location away from adult festivities, they communicated a clear message to us that children were not as important as adults.*

    having opportunities to interact with the whole range of human personalities and age groups, to increase his or her comfort level with a wide range of experiential situations

Self-Esteem

Next on the hierarchy of needs is a parent's longing to help children achieve positive self-esteem. Self-esteem builders are present in every situation a child successfully masters. In most cases, the normal mechanics of living require us to learn how to perform or execute a process. To negotiate successfully in the physical world, a child must learn to turn a knob to open a door, flush a toilet, knead dough, shape a cookie, paste paper together, and balance blocks, to name a few. What you as an adult may take for granted is at some point in a child's life a mystery to be solved. With this awareness, be sensitive and slow-going when the child is confronted with such novel events. Almost everything we do as part of our daily routine is learned and therefore an opportunity for self-esteem building. Note the following ideas.

> *I remember the first time I carried my son Zachary over to a light switch. Flicking it off, I would say "Light off," and in reverse, "Light on." I must have done this at least a dozen times before I took his little hand and had him help me snap the switch on and off. After he had memorized this procedure, I placed a chair below the light switch and encouraged him to climb up and flip the light on and off. His tiny mouth curled upward into a giant smile when he had accomplished it. We had scored a big point for self-esteem.*

Common Environmental Self-Esteem Building Opportunities

using light switches
turning doorknobs
flushing toilets
turning faucets on and off
turning keys in locks
using garage door openers
pouring water from a pitcher into a cup

Additional opportunities for building self-esteem abound. Engage your child in basic home activities. Cooking is a good example. Tasks such as kneading dough, cutting a stick of butter, or stirring cake batter are fraught with pleasure for a child. Below are several tasks your child can help with at an early age.

Common Tasks Offering Self-Esteem Building Opportunities

tearing lettuce
kneading dough
slicing butter with a dull knife
stirring batter
shelling peas
drying pots
setting the table
pasting on paper
painting

building with blocks
digging in the garden
planting seeds
picking flowers
arranging flowers in a vase
watering plants
feeding pets
mopping
sponging

In general, all adult activities can be opportunities for building your child's self-esteem. Children don't negatively respond to an activity unless it frightens them or they perceive that the adult they emulate hates it. If your child won't help you dust or mop, then you have probably transmitted your dislike of this activity.

Children's self-esteem is further broadened when they are allowed to put a personal stamp on some activity. Children will develop basic skills, but not all will perform them in the same way. Even something as routine as brushing your teeth has potential for a great deal of variety. Allow children to perform activities in their own way. So long as your children are not inflicting harm on themselves, allow them to engage in processes in ways that feel natural. Their self-esteem is reinforced whenever children get to arrange, process, and organize things in their physical world uniquely.

To foster their self-esteem, allow your children to

select colors when choosing sheets, blankets, curtains, or wall art for their rooms
decide which toys they want in their crib or bed
dine with adults at the same table
have appropriately sized seats in all gathering spaces
have their favorite items displayed in a family room
choose what clothes to wear
select books they want you to read to them

Self-Actualization

The ultimate test of self is in the arena of actualization. What opportunities exist to facilitate children to become, fully and without impediments, themselves. "Free to Be You and Me," the title of Marlo Thomas's album

When I was a year old I preferred to consume my dinner drinking milk first, then eating the applesauce, and then finally the main course. It drove my mother crazy, since she was of the opinion that the milk and applesauce should be consumed after the main course. She recounts how we would get into a tug of war over what I would eat first. I would gesture toward the milk and applesauce, screaming "Milk, applesauce, meat!" and she would not budge from her perceived proper routine of meat first then other items. At that tender age my chubby calves hung over my shoes, so she couldn't have been worried about my starving to death. Did she fear I would not learn to eat in the proper sequence and be forever a disorganized eater? Did she see this as a battle of control that she wanted to win? Most likely I was thirsty and needed liquid before solids. Some battles just don't need to be fought.

of children's songs, takes place only where children are free to make choices. The first landscape is a home setting, where each child can test his or her way, protected from harm yet unimpeded by unnecessary regulations. Self-actualization flourishes where a child has opportunities to test the waters of diversity, has permission to learn, and is able to self-regulate goals. Self-actualization is the ultimate tool for contentment, for when children are truly able to be themselves, they are shored with an internal strength that enables them to weather even the most stormy of life's passages.

Self-actualization will thrive when opportunities to experiment with many different items, not just toys, exist. Diversity of experience includes being able to learn about, use, and integrate both natural and human-made items. Twigs, water, rocks, leaves, branches, dirt, shells, berries, and critters are some objects found outside that can be brought inside. Pots, pans, towels, sheets, mops, buckets, clocks, pillows, afghans, spoons, paper, safety scissors, pencils, adhesive tape, junk jewelry, hand mufflers, play clothes, and old shoes are just as important as any item on a toy store's shelf. Children's self-actualization thrives when they are allowed to spend as much or as little time with objects as they wish.

Our primitive ancestors needed to spend only three or four days per week engaged in mandatory, life-sustaining activities and used the rest of their time for socialization. Contemporary humans have many more things to take care of and, in spite of all our labor-saving devices, have much less free time. Children feel the effect of the demands of daily life as well as adults. Forcing a child to stay within the confines of time is not always desirable. A healthy person, adult or child, will know when to sleep, how much to eat, and when he or she is tired of an activity. Aside from passive activities such as watching TV, a child will generally juggle enough dissimilar activities in a day to supply sufficient diversity of experience. Within limits, allowing children to self-regulate activities and giving them reasonable decision-making powers, like when to start and stop play, will build their self-esteem and promote self-actualization.

Give your children the opportunity to explore the world around them freely and in a time frame that fits their individual uniqueness. Their self-esteem is shored up by being challenged to acquire more skills in favored areas. The child who thrives on large motor skill activities will find lightweight blocks a fantastic way to explore balance and planning ahead. On the other hand, the child who can line up crumbs on a tray will find dice-sized blocks just right for exploring dexterity. Until we give children the opportunity to explore variety, we may not hit upon their preferred modalities.

Finally, self-actualization is advanced with parental acknowledgment of a child's self-imposed goals. Most parents lavish praise when their child takes his or her first step. Firsts are easy to applaud. But after the first there are a whole host of expressions that are note- and praiseworthy. The fortitude to repeat a practice until it becomes perfect is the stuff of life's many successes.

Before a child can learn to set an entire table, placing a napkin anywhere near a plate is by itself an achievement. Picking up a glass is the goal that preludes drinking from it. A parent's opportunity for goal setting and rewarding are found in tasks later in life that are taken for granted.

STEPS LEADING TO MASTERY	COMPLEX SKILL
Rolling over, holding crib's side bars, balancing on hands and knees	Sitting up
Rocking back and forth on knees, holding onto an item while on knees	Crawling
Crawling, jumping up and down when supported, rolling around in a walker	Standing
Clapping hands, grabbing for an item	Holding a cup or bottle
Gurgling, humming, and making other utterances	Speaking
Pulling apart, unscrewing, filling, and emptying	Comprehending complexity

Providing Good Chi

All chi has potential to be good or bad. Bad chi includes those experiences that do not advance self-esteem, do not create a sense of belonging, do not promote feeling safe, or can cause physical harm. A child who lives in a room with mostly tall pieces of furniture learns to think of him or herself as small and underpowered. The following is a list of potentially negative chi:

high furnishings
corners of furnishings directed toward a child's bed, place at the
     dining table, or play surface
drawers too heavy to open
knobs too big to grasp
slippery flooring
drafts
objects with draped electrical wires

Support activities by incorporating a child's natural chi. For example, if a restless child needs to learn to count, don't force him or her to sit still and learn. Have objects arranged around a room that can be counted, and encourage the child to go and touch each object.

To begin understanding which senses your child uses most when taking in the physical world, observe his reactions to new experiences. When entering a new space, does he move his eyes or head to visually take in the surroundings? Is he riveted by the sound of a person's voice? Is he likely to smell his food before eating it? Is it mandatory to have a "feel good" toy in his crib to cuddle? In the same way you might ask an adult what she would bring if left on a desert island, you should observe what sensory experiences seem essentially comforting or simply are your child's first connection with an environment.

Chi is taken in by the human sensory systems. Assuming all senses are in working order, humans rely most on sight. In childhood, touch or sensory awareness through the skin is more acute than it usually is later on. Consider how some infants may not wake when you speak but will wake after being snuggled. Movement, then sound, and then smell seems to be early childhood's preferential sensory order. Determine the order of relied-upon senses and be sure to provide your child with sufficient stimulation. Below are some examples of extra chi conditions you can provide for children in each sensory category.

Extra Chi Conditions to Provide if Your Child Relies on Sight

unambiguous pathways to activity centers
more than three colors and patterns in a room
a variety of depths (pictures with a vanishing point)

Extra Chi Conditions to Provide if a Child Relies on Touch

at least three different textures of fabrics
    in a setting
at least two layers of flooring materials
    (e.g., area carpet over other flooring)
manipulatives with the consistencies of
    sand, clay, silk, stone, velvet, foam
    rubber, and water

For children who rely on the visual as a way of learning and interacting with an environment, pictures with a depth view can make a space more engaging.

Extra Chi Conditions to Provide if a Child Relies on Movement

an unencumbered pathway or straightaway
furniture positioned to allow the child to encircle it
a mobile that responds to a breeze

Extra Chi Conditions to Provide if a Child Relies on Sound

music and a selection of musical instruments or music-making objects
chimes mounted on the door or near an open window
flooring on which footsteps are audible
a babbling fish tank or fountain

Extra Chi Conditions to Provide if a Child Relies on Smell

pots of fragrant herbs
recirculating water with a seasonal scent added
    • pine or cypress scent in winter
    • earth or crocus scent in spring
    • jasmine or rose scent in summer
    • geranium or pumpkin scent in fall
a selection of potpourri placed inside cupboard, closets, drawers and
    under furniture

Having the fullest tapestry of sensory information reinforces our connection to life. Be sure that the time your child spends indoors is filled with the same sensory variety as that nature provides outdoors. That is the essence of good chi.

5

Elemental, Dear Watson

Feng Shui's Five Elements

Feng shui is based on the principle that there are five elements—fire, earth, metal, water, and wood—defining all of the physical world. Practically everything we see, hear, touch, and smell on earth is a by-product of one or more of feng shui's five elements. These elements define the composition of all content in the physical world, but exclude the animal kingdom. Vegetation, soil, minerals, and natural and manufactured products are made from the five elements and they make up the content of our physical world.

Look around at all the things in your home. All of them are made from either earth, metal, or wood, with plastics being formed from earth and/or metal. Amazing, isn't it? All the hundreds of items surrounding you are generated from three elements: earth, metal, or wood (the wood element represents all things that grow).

The other two elements, fire and water, are the **catalysts** used to shape the content elements. Fire represents actual fire as well as all activities created or shaped by heat. A hand that polishes a stone or saws a plank is indicative of the fire element. Water's action makes objects flexible. Therefore reshaping and stretching materials, bending, pouring, or pulling, is the basic action of the water element. Therefore fire and water are the intrinsic elements that are used to form materials. Fire and water are the catalysts, and earth, metal, and wood are the content; together they contain all that is necessary to forge all objects in the physical world.

Feng Shui Elemental Categories

ELEMENT	DOMAIN OF ELEMENT
Fire	Actual fire and all processes that involve heat, including carving, sawing, slapping, and speed
Earth	Actual earth and all processes that require consolidation, patting, kneading, shaping, and stuffing
Metal	All metals and mineral compounds and all processes that require planning, outwitting, deliberation, and mental manipulation
Water	Actual water and all processes that require bending, pulling, pouring, and filling
Wood	All things that grow and all processes that require changing, learning, growing, and building

All categories have an implicit personality and therefore, like human personalities, can be characterized. Elemental personality descriptions are closely aligned with many personality type theories developed by modern-day psychologists and psychiatrists. In my book *Feng Shui and How to Look Before You Love*, I created self-tests that match a person's behavioral and emotional proclivities to elemental categories. As all parents know, each child has his or her own personal style. Don't try to rush a contemplator or slow down a firebrand. The descriptions below can give you an indication of which elemental category your child falls into. Many children have bits and pieces of more than one category, so don't expect only one element to dominate, although it may. There are visual tests in Chapter 10 to give your child to help you uncover his or her elemental personality.

Fire Personality

Fire children are apt to be active, tear into things, and take risks.

Fire personalities like to be active, reach out before contemplating risks, prefer to whip things around, push toys with wheels, tear into things quickly, and perform most activities with alacrity. If you child drinks with great gulps, expresses frustration overtly and forcefully, and runs rather than walks, you probably have a child possessing a great deal of fire. These children usually are the first to respond to questions and are apt to make their presence known immediately.

Fire kids are quick and crave instant gratification. They tend to vocalize their needs, often loudly. A baby who howls rather than whimpers to express discomfort or displeasure, a toddler who waddles into furniture because he or she moves too quickly, and a young child who'd rather jump up and down than sit still are exhibiting fire traits. As in all elemental categories, there are both positive and challenging attributes. The following is a list of what you might expect if your child has lots of fire in his or her disposition.

Fire Personality Traits

POSITIVE	CHALLENGING
Responsive	Rushes
Enjoys many activities	Easily distracted by another activity
Resists manipulation	Combative
Passionate	Excitable
Charismatic	Needs to be the center of attention

If the **positive** traits of fire are present, support your child by including the following conditions in his or her physical environment:

Conditions Supporting Positive Fire

light colors such as whites, beige, silver, copper, and pale yellow in the bedroom
a square rug or blanket to play on
complex spaces with many options

If your child exhibits some of the more **challenging** traits of fire, you may want to balance these traits by including the following elements in his or her physical environment.

Balancing Challenging Fire

colors of the earth—tan, terra-cotta, taupe, dark beige, sand, adobe, and brown—for flooring, providing a stabilizing play surface
a picture with scenes of the desert, a flat landscape with placid water, or a cave scene hanging across from your child's dining seat
navy blue or charcoal gray in the bedroom
a very large table surface to play on
use few primary colors, especially with crisp contrasts

Earth Personality

Earth children are methodical and feel secure with the familiar.

An earth child might hide behind the legs of his parents, reach for objects slowly and methodically, keep a hand over her mouth after placing food there, or sit in the middle of a blanket or play area without straying from its border. All processes that include consolidation, patting, kneading, shaping, and stuffing and do not call forth quick physical responses are comfortable for children with an earth bent. Earth children desire things to remain the same. Not necessarily shy, children with earth personalities are simply more comfortable with the tried and true than with the new or innovative. Don't expect these children to give up old toys or try new foods easily, for earth children feel secure with repetition and the familiar.

Earth Personality Traits

POSITIVE	CHALLENGING
Willing to try	Shies away from new situations
Realistic goal setting	Underestimates own ability
Loyal	Hesitates to interact with unfamiliar people
Careful	Stubborn
Explores in depth	Unwilling to part with things
Strives for harmony in groups	Tends to separate self from groups

If the **positive** traits of earth are present, support your child by including the following conditions in his or her physical environment:

Conditions Supporting Positive Earth

colors of wine, magenta, or russet in the bedroom
a round table to play at
uncluttered space
a painting with lots of green vegetation in his or her bedroom or
     across from his or her dining seat

If your child exhibits some of the more **challenging** traits of earth, you may want to balance these traits by including the following elements in his or her physical environment:

Balancing Challenging Earth

royal blue or turquoise bedsheets
clouds or a sky scene painted on the child's bedroom ceiling
furniture covering or a blanket with red stripes
a metallic frame around bedroom artwork
a flashlight positioned near the bed

Metal Personality

If your child's favorite game is hide-and-seek, if she rarely lets you leave her bedside without reading and explaining stories, if jigsaw puzzles are her favorite toy, and every day she invents new ways to use things, then you probably have sired a metal personality. Metal is the element of the mind, and children with this inclination love activities in which the player must outwit, figure out, or plan ahead. Chess players typically have a great deal of metal in their personalities, as do scholars, pure research scientists, and writers. Any activity that requires an individual to consolidate, think, define, extract, or extrapolate is considered a metal activity. If most of your child's sentences or conversations end with a question mark, then she has metal in her personality configuration.

Metal children think, research, and investigate.

Metal Personality Traits

POSITIVE	CHALLENGING
Thorough	Defensive
Aboundingly curious	Obsessive about having to know details
Serious	Emotionally unavailable
Focused	Unresponsive to others' needs
Discerning	Picky

If the **positive** traits of metal are present, support your child by including the following conditions in his or her physical environment:

Conditions Supporting Positive Metal

medium and light blues, pale turquoise, salmon, pink, and purple
for the bedroom

fabric patterns with undulating lines
individual lamps along with ceiling lights
a picture of a seascape hanging across from his or her dining seat

If your child exhibits some of the more **challenging** traits of metal, you may want to balance these traits by including the following elements in his or her physical environment.

Balancing Challenging Metal
absence of all shiny surfaces, including glossy paint
no dots or circles on fabrics
toys with few wheels or movable parts
cushy, plush seating

Water Personality

Water children are self-sufficient, emotional, and compassionate.

Is your child a dreamer? Does he commonly stare off into space or look at you without listening? If small slights induce tears, and feelings are easily hurt, yet being loving comes easily, then you are living with a child of the water element. A water personality is likely to be self-sufficient yet have a hard time controlling emotions. The child who weeps but doesn't want intervention is exhibiting water's duality. Later in life this child will probably be the one friends unburden themselves to, for a water personality overflows with compassion. Interest in physical things is overshadowed by interest in people; therefore a water child may be late acquiring physical skills. Since a water personality is likely to be uncommonly attentive to the feelings of others, your child may appear not to require much maintenance.

Water Personality Traits

POSITIVE	CHALLENGING
Flexible	Emotionally needy
Accepting	Gives in to others
Undauntedly persistent	Bulldozes past others' needs
Pensive	Secretive and unavailable
Respectful of property and others	Xenophobic

If the **positive** traits of water are present, support your child by including the following conditions in his or her physical environment.

Conditions Supporting Positive Water

white bedroom or playroom walls
undressed windows
shelving on walls in bedroom
a wall hanging with a geometric pattern hanging across from his or
    her dining seat or bed

If your child exhibits some of the more **challenging** traits of water, you may want to balance these traits by including the following elements in his or her physical environment.

Balancing Challenging Water

bed linens with stars, triangles, or diamond patterns
jasmine, geranium, lemon, or grapefruit scents in the play areas
a cuckoo clock, door chimes, or other intermittent sounds
absence of silky, smooth fabrics; presence of linen or natural cotton
    fabrics

Wood Personality

Exploring is the key activity of a wood child. This personality type loves adventures, although many exploits are perceived by parents as involving a high level of risk. Undaunted by the unfamiliar, a wood child is exhilarated by learning. What constitutes pressure for the other types of personalities is easy for wood children to withstand. Pressure to perform quickly or finish up is comfortable for wood children, who are barely able to finish one task because the next one beckons them. A wood personality will often try to perform gross motor feats even if not developmentally ready. For example, a wood infant might prop himself up to peer around even though his head is bobbing because his neck muscles aren't ready to support the head. It is very hard for wood children to follow instructions because they are usually already immersed in the task. Generally truthful and often impatient, they are almost powerless to resist a tremendous urge to act.

Wood children are exhilarated by learning.

Wood Personality Traits

Positive	Challenging
Adventurous	Demanding
Willing to take chances	Takes dangerous risks
Unique	Impulsive
Loves new tasks	Tends not to complete tasks
Action oriented	Powerless to stop

If the **positive** traits of wood are present, support your child by including the following conditions in his or her physical environment.

Conditions Supporting Positive Wood

striped bedsheets

plants to care for

your acceptance of all the clutter your wood child is likely to spread around

lots of outdoor activities

room available for lots of projects out all at once

If a child exhibits some of the more **challenging** traits of wood, you may want to balance these traits by including the following conditions in his or her physical environment.

Balancing Challenging Wood

use few fabrics with bold contrasts

use little red, wine, brown, and russet with blues for the bedroom

a variety of low surfaces on which to perch and play

don't select striped fabrics

paintings having lots of whites and metal colors, or with metallic mats or frames, seen from his or her dining seat or bed

Elemental Categories Relating to Age of Child

Along with a child's individual nature, the developmental stages discussed in Chapter 2 of this book are each aligned with an elemental category. In the following sections I will discuss the Me, Myself, and I stage; the Magician stage; and the On the Road to Reason stage as they relate to their dominating elements, water, metal, and wood, respectively.

The Me, Myself, and I Stage (Birth to Eighteen Months): Water Element

An infant emerges from the ultimate water environment, and slowly over the span of this stage emerges into an environment that supports life in an entirely different way. The younger the child, the narrower the separation is from the perceived universe and the notion of self. Therefore, birth to eighteen months is the stage of swimming in life's substances or feeling immersed inside a great wave. As an infant becomes more aware and learns to identify the surroundings, the bubble of water in which the infant resides starts to dissolve.

Underwater nothing is sharp or extreme, sounds are muffled, light is diffused, and scents are almost nonexistent. A water environment envelops the senses and cocoons the soul. It supports rather than jars and gently coaxes an infant to enter the world.

In order to nurture a child of the age group of birth to eighteen months, try to simulate such a water environment. Here are some further suggestions on how to do this.

Suggestions for an Infant's Water Environment

patterns with small repeats

pale, muted, or dark colors; avoid primary colors

pools of light not aimed directly at the infant

sheer curtains diffusing direct sunlight

cushioned upholstery on furnishings and a yielding, carpeted floor surface

pliant bedding

cool temperatures

distinct contrast

harp or other stringed instrument music

The colors of water are blue and black and muted, not shiny. Water textures have depth or are open weave so that they invite tactile investigation. The smells are blends of all that exists, like the scent of earth. Earthy scents exude from infants' bodies, and these scents appear comforting to them. Certainly antiseptic, biting scents normally associated with cleaning fluids are the antithesis of a water atmosphere. Music of the harp, violin, or any other stringed instrument, whose sounds reverberate in the air waves, fading away naturally rather than abruptly, are inherently closer to the water element than any other tones.

The Magician Stage (Eighteen Months to Three Years): Metal Element

"What?" "Who?" "Why?" This is the litany of a child entering into the Magician stage. The child begins to comprehend, however reluctantly, that the world is, in fact, a separate entity. At approximately eighteen months of age the facility of discernment develops. Newly formed is the ability to extrapolate, and mental processes expand exponentially. During this stage, the child will learn to identify most items in his or her physical world and understand their purpose and use. It takes a great deal of mental concentration to be able to learn so many things in such a short period of time. In fact, the volume of information processed later in life probably never approaches the amount absorbed at this stage of life.

Concentration and mental acuity is the hallmark of the metal element. Since many experiences are either new or newly acquired, the Magician is often very intense. I have observed children during this stage stare fiercely at something while trying to figure it out. How different from the wandering, completely unpredictable stare of an infant, who gazes around as if waking up from a long slumber! Inference, deduction, and reckoning are abilities of the metal element, when discernment is used in understanding all the sensory input from the physical world.

Because the age of eighteen months to three years is fraught with experimentation, it is the responsibility of parents to expose children to new experiences, tastes, sounds, scents, and concrete objects. The more exposure, the more mastery of life in general. Wise parents provide an environment that will nurture the Magician, who will flourish with metal elements in his or her environment that take into account his or her individual nature.

Excitement compels many parents to lavish all kinds of toys on their newborn, but the real trick is how to keep this up during the Magician stage without living in a complete disaster zone. For a metal environment, a child should be surrounded by a variety of toys and provided with diversity of experiences, yet not expected to keep things in order. A parent has to be patient and respect a child's limitations in this regard. My only advice is don't despair; this stage doesn't last forever.

Gold, white, silver, copper, and any reflective surface are good metal colors. Metal's shape is a circle (hence the fascination with wheels by so many at this age), the textures are smooth or wet, and sound is the music of a guitar, xylophone, or piano.

Because this stage is dominated by the metal element, the Magician would rather focus on minutia and ignore social interaction. Everything is fascinating to the Magician, and it's hard for the child not to be transfixed by whatever interests him or her. The fun games during this stage involve somewhat slippery objects that are challenging to hold, the way a drop of mercury eludes picking up. Here are some suggestions for conditions to include.

Suggestions for a Magician Metal Environment

patterns with repeats
reflective surfaces
mid-tone colors of terra-cotta, pink, beige, and yellow
window coverings that let in outside light (e.g., slatted blinds,
     perforated fabrics)
resistant surfaces
rounded corners on furnishings
diverse bedding (e.g., different-sized blankets, pillows, stuffed animals)
a variety of objects to manipulate

On the Road to Reason Stage (Three to Six Years): Wood Element

Gaining mastery is the essence of the On the Road to Reason stage. Simple curiosity to the desire to fully understand in order to create is the hallmark of wood. The hit-or-miss approach of the two year old gives way to the planned activities of the three year old. It is during this stage that the light bulb goes on inside the child's brain with the discovery that there is always more to learn. This stage is best spiced with diversity, challenges, and learning.

Developing abstract ideas and converting them to another form is an essential life tool. Many of a child's first memories stem from this time, and what a child learns during this explosive learning stage is often linked to who he or she will be as an adult. The wood element's status quo is change. A sense of identity springs forth in this stage, as a child begins to look like what he or she will become as an adult.

> *I remember wanting to be the "tough guy," protecting my neighborhood friends from a bully's threats. When the "terminator" came barreling down the street, it was me who tossed caution aside and stepped in front of his speeding bike to halt his approach. Probably the sight of my roly-poly, grimacing four-year-old face was sufficiently startling to arrest the forward motion of this six-year-old pest. It was as if a light bulb was lit that day, for I realized that I was capable of standing up for what I wanted.*

In the On the Road to Reason stage, children consciously figure out who they are and what options feel comfortable for them.

Children are inspired to learn when there is room to explore at will. When a child's life is overfilled with "should"s and "ought to"s, the emergence of selfhood may be stifled. All things grow up or out, vertically or horizontally, and when there is no room for expansion, a shape or spirit becomes misshapen and compromised. One way to support opportunities for new interests is to grant a child empty spaces. Just like a diary's empty pages invite authorship, vacant spaces supply a canvas for a child's imagination. Along with empty spaces, environments stimulating growth and change are appropriate for the wood stage. Following are some conditions that help foster such environments.

Suggestions for the Road to Reason's Wood Environment

striped wallpapers
a wall, a floor, or bedding
   with a profusion of greens
playthings that bounce or can
   be bounced on

blankets of all shapes, colors,
   and sizes
bath toys and accessories
cleared counter surfaces
window shades with cutouts

toys that can be taken apart and put back together teepees, tents, playhouses	flashlights thick, small area rugs stools that swivel

⑨   ⑨   ⑨

In conclusion, it is important to create an environment for your child that will stimulate the desire for appropriate change. For example, heavy chairs that are hard to drag can frustrate a child and prevent him or her from moving them to create a variety of play situations. Stippled or sponged surfaces can stimulate diverse mental activities in your child like the cloud formations you peered at as a child that featured kangaroos leaping or faces peering down at you. Plants perched in front of windows cast shadows, and perforated lampshades throwing patterns of light can be part of the melange of shapes delighting a child as he or she dances On the Road to Reason.

6

The Ba-Gua

The Implied Meaning of Space

The *ba-gua* is a feng shui tool that reveals the emotional communications generated by different parts of a space. In pyramid feng shui the ba-gua is used room by room more frequently than throughout the entire house as a single entity because one experiences a space more fully when present in it. Although the ba-gua is often represented as an eight-sided shape, it is really the same shape as the room over which it is applied.

The traditional ba-gua has nine segments, but a child's interaction with the world is not quite that specific. For our purposes in this book, I have consolidated the segments into five comprehensive areas: motivation, power, challenge, relationships, and health. These five areas give you a template for planning activities appropriately.

In order to locate the various sections of the ba-gua, stand at the entrance to a room, the door or threshold most frequently used. The power wall is usually straight ahead, but not always; mitigating features such as no wall along one side of a room because it connects with another, a row of windows on one side, or special features such as a fireplace change the locations of the room's ba-gua areas.

Traditional ba-gua

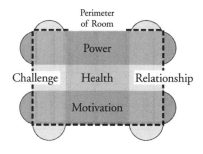

These five areas reveal a child's communication with a space.

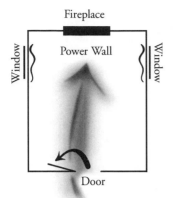

The power wall is straight ahead on the room's main pathway.

Based on the traditional ba-gua, the power wall of the room in the picture on the left would be straight ahead. However, it is unlikely that a person entering this room would move directly ahead; typically people don't walk that close to a wall. When entering a room, we tend to veer toward the largest volume of space. In this room the fireplace wall would be where one is likely to turn after entering. Thus the experiential entrance of this room is facing the fireplace. To map individual rooms, superimpose the ba-gua entrance based on the path a person is likely to take when proceeding into a room, not necessarily the position faced at the entrance. The power wall is always straight ahead after you've determined that point.

Motivation

What enchants a child? What ingredients send thoughts swirling? What toys are so favored that the mere mention of them is thrilling? Children respond quickly to enthusiasm, and the motivation area of a room generates eagerness. A child can be gently prodded toward many moods, and what is experienced at the threshold holds the key.

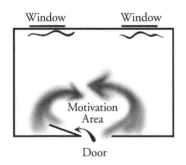

The motivation area is just inside the threshhold.

Motivation Area

What to Include

ICON	BENEFIT
A mobile that flutters gently	Aids rest
A gyrating spiral	Stimulates action
An area rug	Emanates support
Low lighting	Invites introspection
A sturdy piece of furniture	Bestows security

What to Avoid

ICON	DISADVANTAGE
Clutter	Advances confusion
Intense lighting	Garners attention too immediately
Only adult possessions	Devalues self-esteem
Emptiness (especially in bedrooms)	Depletes a sense of possibilities

Power

All people feel safer when they are against a contiguous wall farthest from the entrance to a space. Therefore, activities requiring concentration and focus are best located against the power wall. You will be encouraging your child to spend more time engaged in activities that build self-esteem when you locate these activities in the power area. If a television is placed against this wall, you will imbue it with even more allure.

Power Area

What to Include

Icon	Benefit
Sofa or other seating facing the entrance	Enhances the feeling of protection and safety
Books and toys	Enhances the value of learning by reading and doing
Bed	Provides protection
Set of blocks	Encourages risk taking
Mechanical or intricate games or activities	Sharpens focus
Pet cages	Intensifies the value of caring

What to Avoid

Icon	Disadvantage
Television	Encourages passivity, not involvement
Solitary seating	Fosters isolation
Emptiness	Increases sense of boredom

Relationship

The vast majority of humans are right-side dominant. Scientists have discovered that left-handedness is caused by hormonal changes in utero; therefore, most left-handed people were originally right-side dominant. What that means in terms of feng shui is people tend to move to the right more frequently than they do toward the left when entering a space. Thus the right side of a space feels more natural to go toward, and is the preferred and more comforting side to proceed to when entering a space.

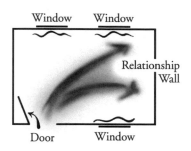

Locate places to meet with people on the right-hand side of the room.

Relationship Area

What to Include

ICON	BENEFIT
Bed	Lessens fear of being alone
Two chairs at right angles	Encourages communication
Sofa	Facilitates alliances
Game or dining table	Fosters togetherness
Play area with activities requiring cooperation	Harnesses teamwork

What to Avoid

ICON	DISADVANTAGE
Solitary chair	Exacerbates feeling of isolation
Computer	Undermines togetherness
Solo activities	Isolates and disconnects
Entertainment center	Will emphasize being entertained rather than entertaining oneself

Challenge

The challenge area is left of the entrance. Often what we struggle with initially becomes our greatest achievement. Without challenge even the most talented children may not fulfill their promise. If someone had told me I would be a writer in high school, I would have fallen off my desk chair. My family nickname was Miss Malaprop, and I didn't know the fabric of syntax from a synthetic fabric. Although I loved penning rhymes for family events, the longer versions of writing were fraught with mistakes in spelling and grammar. The kid who couldn't write a complete sentence is today writing her seventh book.

Challenge is among the most important tools parents can supply their child with. Meeting challenges is key in shaping life's worth.

The puzzle for parents to figure out is what to place in the challenge section of their child's room. Place something

Tasks that require focus are supported in the challenge area.

One of my female cousins was by far the most beautiful and talented member of my extended family. There wasn't an art form she didn't excel in. She could draw, dance, act, play piano, and sing. She rode horses with great confidence, got jokes quicker than others, and frolicked in water as if she were born there. I felt like a complete dud next to her. I loved to draw, but my pictures were clumsy and were smudged with drips of paint. My enthusiasm for singing was great until a teacher asked me to lip-sync in the all-school choir. I used to long to be like my talented, beautiful cousin—until I became an adult. Since the only way I could succeed was to apply myself, I was motivated to conquer what I enjoyed. My cousin never achieved the kind of success and contentment her talents promised. Because of her abundant talents she wasn't motivated to strive for achievement.

compelling in the challenge area. Locate a more advanced version of your child's favorite activity in the challenge area. For example, if a two year old plays happily with a ten-piece puzzle, place a twenty-piece puzzle there, too.

Challenge Area

What to Include

ICON	BENEFIT
The next level of toys and games	Challenges and sets goals
Plants to tend to	Inspires consistency
Puzzles	Encourages the completion of tasks
Open toy shelves or bookshelves	Exhibits options

What to Avoid

ICON	DISADVANTAGE
Cluttered toys or games	Overwhelms
A dresser or closed storage	Supplies opportunity for suppressing
Emptiness (especially in the bedroom)	Offers no stimulation
Any tasks that the child dislikes	Exacerbates conflict and negativity

Health

The center of a room represents all aspects of health. In my other books on feng shui, I explain health as physical, mental, and spiritual health. With children spiritual health is also associated with feelings of being nurtured and protected by family. Therefore a defined and easy-to-identify center is preferred in rooms for children. A center can be something as simple as an area rug in a bedroom or a coffee table/play surface in the family room. Like a hug, when a room's central area is defined, it transmits to children a feeling of being cared for and loved.

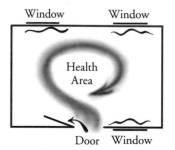

Define the center of a child's room as the health area.

Health Area

What to Include

ICON	BENEFIT
Your child's favorite play materials	Honors a child's preferences
Area rug	Provides a clear circumference
Blanket	Comforts
Sufficient and bright lighting	Adds significance to activities

What to Avoid

ICON	DISADVANTAGE
Emptiness	Diffuses sense of security
Toy chest	Overemphasizes children
Only adult accessories	Overemphasizes adults
Solitary chair	Puts too much pressure on occupant

The Four Corners

The areas where two sections converge hold the energy of both segments. These corners are the four human tools for self-empowerment. For example, the space on the furthermost right-hand side is the one in which a child would feel safest and most supported by family because it is the segment of a room where relationships and power meet. When the appropriate items are placed in this area, feelings of intimacy are sparked and a child feels nurtured by the activity he or she is engaged in.

⑨   ⑨   ⑨

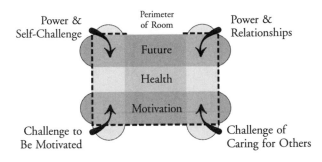

The areas where two sections converge hold the energy of both segments and are the four human tools for self-empowerment.

Use the ba-gua's areas to locate various activity centers and furnishings and as a tool for customizing a home to fit an individual child's needs. Like all feng shui tools, ba-gua should be used in conjunction with the others. If, for example, you realize that an entertainment unit is in a location that is not ideal, don't panic. Consider how to make a room in a room. To create a space within space, use placement of furniture, area carpets, or other accessories such as screens, plants, or tables to shape an interior space, thereby mitigating the larger, less auspicious placement.

Consider how important the aspects of the ba-gua are throughout life. When our children are motivated and empowered to meet challenges and are supported by healthy, loving relationships, then their lives become rich with possibilities. By supporting these aspects, parents transmit the tools that will serve their children throughout their lifetimes. What better gift can parents bestow?

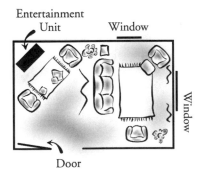

Use the placement of furniture, carpets, and screens to create a room within a room if necessary.

7

Color Me Happy

We rely on sight more than any other sense to secure information about our surroundings. Because our species sees a greater variety of colors than other species do, the influence of color on our psyche is vast.

The Meaning of Colors

Colors have inherent meanings, and understanding what each color communicates is an important step when selecting colors for a child's environment. Color Chart is a handy reference guide to selecting colors. Be sure to pair this information with your child's elemental preferences for the best results.

Green

If I were to pick one color to represent childhood, it would be green. Green is the color of growth, change, evolution, and emergence. Like children, vegetation grows miraculously before our eyes. Seeds planted in the earth quickly germinate and sprout into saplings. Trees transform themselves yearly and renew their crowns each spring. In no time weedy growth can obliterate an unattended garden. You can't think about vegetation without admiring its ability to renew, grow, and change.

Consider what makes a plant green. The enzyme chlorophyll that converts the sun's energy into sugar is green. Chlorophyll's role in a plant's life cycle centers around sustaining growth. On a very primal level green does

Color Chart

COLOR	ELEMENT	POSITIVE CONSEQUENCE	CHALLENGING CONSEQUENCE
Primary Colors			
Deep red	Fire	Inspires activity	Inhibits falling asleep
Pink	Fire	Calms	Stimulates restlessness
Deep yellow	Earth	Secures clarity	Invites disassociation
Light yellow	Earth	Cheers	Summons risk taking
Deeply reflective	Metal	Fosters concentrating	Deters interacting
Lightly reflective	Metal	Energizes	Can unveil too many options
Deep blue	Water	Helps focus on self	Can exacerbate gloom
Light blue	Water	Aids in self-expression	May exacerbate self-centeredness
Deep green	Wood	Spurs exploring	Contributes to noncompletion of tasks
Light green	Wood	Aids emotional development	May intensify fickleness
Other Colors			
Turquoise	Wood/water	Envelops with confidence	Causes emotional divisiveness
Orange	Fire/earth	Stimulates family bonds	Promotes over-attachments
Purple	Fire/water	Activates internal conversation	Disconnects from being present
Brown	Earth/fire	Envelops with security	Muffles innovations and change
Black	Water/water	Stimulates the imagination	Intimidates or frightens

not exude dormancy. I mention this because so many people erroneously believe that green has a calming effect. In fact, the mistaken notion that green is a relaxing color is based in part on its association with nature. What is confusing is that we feel relaxed when in a natural setting because all senses are engaged. Looking at green doesn't replicate that entire experience. Because it is the catalyst for growth, change, and transformation green is fundamentally invigorating, not relaxing.

Change can be the impetus for all meaningful, positive contributions in life, or it can mean the kind of bone-numbing, stomach-churning adjustments that are caused by shock, distress, loss, or trauma. A negative reaction to change of movement is seasickness, which makes us turn green. The expression "green with envy" is used to describe someone with the desire to possess another's characteristics—that is, fundamentally change himself or herself. In real and more abstract ways the color green resonates with an affinity for, comfort with, or need for growth, change, exploration, adventure, and variation and the discomfort with the static, the repetitive, the stationary. Green can help a child reach goals, or if misapplied can slip him or her into the vilest stranglehold. What parents need to be aware of is when the energy of change is appropriate and necessary for a child's specific circumstance and personality.

Green May Be Appropriate

- when a child overemphasizes one activity
- when a child is fearful of venturing out
- when a child clings too fervently to caretakers
- for a child who is temperamentally laid back
- when a child spends most of his or her time with adults
- to encourage a child to learn new skills
- when a child needs a boost of energy

Green May Be Inappropriate

- when a new sibling arrives
- during a divorce period
- if a child can't slow down or relax easily
- for a child who has sleep problems

Patrick was born relaxed. Patrick is the first child and may remain the only one for his forty-something parents. Both parents work, and until just after his second birthday, he was cared for at home by a loving nanny. Adults had dominated Patrick's experiences until this time, when his nanny became sick. Overnight Patrick began preschool. Adding some green in his bedroom at this time would reinforce the change he must make. For an only child with a gentle temperament, a dominant green theme can provide the catalyst for appropriate inner growth.

Barnaby, on the other hand, has lived in a very different world. Born seven years after his older sister, Barnaby arrived winking and laughing at life. I always feel that Barnaby gets the joke before I do and believes adults, in general, are just too slow-witted to pick up the subtleties he observes. Adults and children of all ages swoosh through his home on a regular basis. While both parents work, they do so at different times so that his primary caretakers are his mother, father, or occasionally his sister, one of which is always present. Living in a family-oriented neighborhood, children of all ages are easily accessible and encouraged to visit. Barnaby has a tough time going to bed, mainly because he hates to miss anything. Therefore, green in his room would be the antithesis of what he needs to balance his already highly stimulating, growth-oriented life.

The day Kelly's dad moved out, she became sick. At five years old, she was unable to articulate the turmoil and pain she felt. Kelly had begun a rampage of throwing away toys and losing things like her galoshes, umbrella, lunch box, and favorite games. What had been infrequent episodes became the norm after her dad left.

Kelly had always loved the color green and had associated it with her name. Her mom used to tell Kelly how much she loved the color since her college blazer had been kelly green. Not surprisingly, Kelly's bedroom was painted green. Her mother asked me to evaluate their home from a feng shui perspective, with special attention to helping mother and daughter cope with the transition, I was immediately concerned about the color of Kelly's room. Kelly showed all the behavior of the challenging side of green, yet she associated herself positively with this color.

I suggested to Kelly's mom that she remove green from Kelly's field of vision while in bed or when at her frequently used play location. Kelly liked to spend a good deal of time alone in her room. Thus green, the color that accentuates change and growth has the capacity to help a person feel connected or disconnected. At this time green was not a good choice. The changes experienced by Kelly were heightened by the large doses of green.

The green walls were painted a soothing, light rosy tan hue, and a bluish turquoise easily covered up the dark green trim. Kelly kept her green pillowcase and bottom sheet, but we changed the top sheet from green to pink. Her green wicker rocking chair was spray-painted a light peach, and generally her room took on a more buoyant atmosphere. Her negative reactions to change abated over time, melting away as the colors were changed from the ones that activated the wrenching experience of change to those that soothed and lightened Kelly's emotional load.

When used appropriately, green can be the impetus to a love of learning, inventing, and changing, freely allowing your child's spirit to move through. But when it is necessary to pull in the reins and control behavior, green may stand in the way.

Red

Call it blood, crimson, maroon, cherry, rose, mauve, or hibiscus, all shades of red send out vibrations that swirl in space like fluttering ribbons strung from a ceiling fan. Red is associated with anger, intensity, virility, animation, charisma, and power. Red conjures up physical energy and intense emotion. Consider how many countries choose to include red in their flags and national symbols. Think about the plethora of family crests, symbols of success, and sport uniforms that are emblazoned with this color. Why is this so?

Physiologically, red is associated with many strong reactions, and its wavelength is the longest in the visible light spectrum. Not only is red's wave long, but it pulses at a slower speed than other colors. It's more like a flag fluttering in a light breeze than one whipping around in gale-force winds. Red's cadence commands attention like a persistent, resonant voice amid high-pitched chatter. Just as we can't ignore the tenacity of a metronome, we acknowledge red instinctively.

Red howls out for attention. It animates. It is a carrier of excitement and zeal and activates or enlivens the pace of activities. Do not use too much red when tranquility, introspection, and decorum are needed.

Expressions like "red-hot" and "red with anger" capture red's association with heat and fire. In the context of red's connection to fire, it is easy to understand that red generates an extreme, intense reaction to one's environment. Being caught "red handed," having to endure "a red-eye flight," or uncovering "a red herring" communicate other associations such as shame, exhaustion, or oddness, all of which connote an extreme result of an event.

Red is an acknowledgment of childhood's high energy and desire to soak up knowledge while being in a state of flux. When anger or unrestrained and inappropriate physical actions are present, red is not beneficial.

Red May Be Appropriate

- to earmark a special occasion
- to signal special attention
- to spark the desire to learn
- to stimulate physical activity
- to encourage loquaciousness

Red May Be Inappropriate

- for a physically overactive child
- when bedrest and quiet is desired
- when a child easily becomes angry and frustrated
- when a child sleeps fitfully
- when a child needs time to absorb before acquiring skills

Chloe's personality is a rare combination of shyness and drama. Until she was seven she was tentative about engaging in physical activities. But when an opportunity for mental risk taking arose, she would excitedly venture anything. Too much red in her case would encourage her tendency to get lost in her imagination at the expense of physical activity. Since red is a color that spurs on physical, mental, or emotional activity, a child with a clear propensity for any one of these can be stymied from entering the less preferred areas when surrounded by red.

Chad developed quietly. All his newly acquired skills did not erupt like a volcano, bursting into existence one day, but rather like a vine creeping over a fence, bit by bit. If this type of child had too much red in his environment, it might create a sense of anxiety and interfere with his natural pace of development. Red underscores a sense of urgency, and if your child is like the tortoise, slow but steady, too much red can be denying of his or her true self. There is, however, always a place for red in a child's spaces. Scattered bits of red stimulate exploration.

Blue

Who is not charmed and awed by a star-studded night? In his painting *Starry Night* (1889) famous Dutch painter Vincent van Gogh (1853–1890) stroked swirls of cloud wisps over a passionate blue sky; the dynamics of line and the breadth of blues transfix us. The sky has always been a source of wonder. Serving as humanity's early navigation system, this expanse of blue and black has provided the information with which to explore distant lands and safely return home. Even today, distant planets, stars, and galaxies are where our collective consciousness converges in awe.

Because the sky's blue is reflected in all bodies of water, we see vast amounts of this color. What does expansiveness and awareness of unknowingness mean intrinsically to the human psyche? The source of human wonder lies in the unraveling of life's mysteries. And what could be more mysterious and consequential to us than knowledge of self? Were one word assigned as a meaning to blue, it would be *self*.

Homo sapiens is the only species whose knowledge of death ingrains in the living an isolation so deep that its only remedy is to uncover meaning in the here and now. While children in early childhood don't muse about the meaning of death, the color blue still evokes the mystery inherent in being alive in them. Faber Birren, whose books on color examine its effects on human experience, points out that a room painted blue actually lowers blood pressure and pulse rates of test subjects. Blue is calming, relaxing, and soothing.

On the other hand, blue may communicate complacency, weariness, and emptiness, evoking melancholy, the feeling of being all alone in the world.

The color blue has the subconscious advantage of building self-esteem and disadvantage of isolating the child who feels adrift. Unless accented by other colors, a blue color scheme is not a good choice for early-childhood spaces. As in all cases, there are exceptions: a colicky or overactive child may benefit from exposure to a dominant scheme of blue.

Blue May Be Appropriate

- to temper a high level of activity
- to build self-esteem
- to help with focus
- to cool down a child who tends to get overheated
- to honor or single out

Blue May Be Inappropriate

- when a child is too sedentary
- when a child is prone to irritability or sadness
- if a child is fearful
- when a child is often alone
- when a child typically feels chilly

At three and a half Michael was a human tornado. Every waking minute his body was in motion. His sedate, gentle mother's intervention seemed irrelevant. On top of this, she was pregnant and hoped that Michael would show more restraint when the new baby arrived. She just couldn't see how to deal with both Michael and a new baby. I suggested a complete sensorial yin intervention, which included using blue as much as possible in all Michael's activity areas.

Now, changing the colors in a child's world doesn't automatically alter his behavior, but like preventing an overactive child from ingesting sugar, every consideration geared to support adjustments will help. Since his behavior was so extreme, sound, scent, and touch needed adjustment to yin. A medium blue is the quintessential yin color, which fosters self-control, tempers physical activity, and generally enhances slowing down.

At four years old, Elizabeth always seemed cranky. While most children her age are easily charmed, she was a tough cookie when it came to amusing her. Elizabeth probably had decided early on that it was useless to try to compete with her dazzling older sister and adopted a contrary posture. (It is not within my expertise to evaluate why a condition exists psychologically, but sometimes I just can't help venturing a guess.) At any rate, what was significant in Elizabeth's case was this: she was grumpy most of the time and a blue-and-green-patterned quilt with a backdrop of light blue walls were not helping. Although blue can build self-esteem, it also can isolate and make a person feel emotionally and physically cold. Elizabeth needed colors with more emotional warmth, colors like yellow, terracotta, and red.

Yellow

Yellow's emotional benefits harmonize with early childhood. Yellow is the color of illumination and clarity and exalts the way a healthy child sees the world. Cultural values and parental dictates are not firmly set at an early age; a yellow environment can serve to clarify taught values and rules. Later in life, when we have to compromise experiences to conform to cultural dictates, we lose a liking for the color yellow.

Putting a great deal of yellow around a talkative child might interfere with her ability to listen. Since yellow charges or sparks optimistic thoughts, too much of it for such a child could cause her to spin out of control. If you have a bubbly, vibrant child, you do not need a large amount of yellow in his or her bedroom, gathering space, or at the family's dining table.

Give children in any culture a directive to draw a picture that includes the sun, and they will consistently select the color yellow to represent it.

In reality the sun is whiter than the vibrant yellow typically selected by children. Yet whether actual or metaphorical, light and clarity are associated with yellow. It is not an accident of nature that there are yellow cells in our eyes called the *macula lutea* that account for visual acuity.

All colors resonate with their use in nature, and humans "get it" subconsciously. Since dying leaves are often pale yellow, this shade is analogous to the process of decay. Childhood is associated with development, not decay. Therefore pass over pale yellow for the rooms of children who are isolated from other children; it can exacerbate feelings of loneliness.

Bright yellow defines and cheers. During times of turmoil or upheaval, as with a divorce or the arrival of a new sibling, yellow can help a child deal with emotions while increasing the feeling of well-being. It is hard for a normal child to stay grouchy for long when outside on a sunny day. Additionally, bright yellows are good to use when a child has to be confined, for it helps volumes of time become more tolerable. Remember: a child's perception of time is different from adults'; what is to an adult a short period of time can seem like eternity to a child. The color yellow, like playing outside in sunny daylight, is an antidote to time standing still. Whether a child is recuperating from a weeklong flu or the family is taking a long car trip, using yellow blankets, pillows, or toys can help mitigate irritability.

Yellow May Be Appropriate

- to cheer
- to support clarity of expression
- to counter feelings of isolation

Yellow May Be Inappropriate

- with an overly talkative child
- when a child lives alone with older adults
- in the bedroom of an only child
- a sickroom (pale yellow)

At four years old Barbara suffered a rare disease and had to be kept at home away from other children for long stretches of time. Needless to say, the burden of the disease and the isolation it imposed were not a good combination. The best advice I could offer Barbara's mother was to dramatically alter her room during the periods of confinement. I advised her to have ready in the wings a grab bag of pleasurable, fun things that involved much sensory interaction. In addition, I asked her mother to make a bright yellow poster board sun and tape it on Barbara's window. Loving the idea that yellow could cheer her daughter, Barbara's mom thought of attaching yellow ribbons to the ceiling fan. When the fan was on, the ribbons danced on the ceiling, bringing a joyful tempo to her sickroom.

Orange

A combination of fiery red and optimistic yellow, orange exudes the essence of positive communication, fusion, and cooperation.

In blended households orange can be used to help form a needed bridge between the two families. Children under three typically don't need much help befriending a stepsibling, but often problems arise with older children. A blended family's using orange in the dining or gathering room may lead to more cooperation and acceptance with greater ease. A hazy line exists between the need for adding orange when fusing two families together and eliminating orange when a child suffers from anxiety of separation from a biological parent. In that case orange can magnify a loss. Although feng shui isn't the only tool to use when emotional problems emerge, creating an environment that supports restoring your child's equilibrium can help you achieve desired results.

Orange does not encourage individuality. It is not an accident that the robes of Buddhist monks are orange. What would more precisely express their tradition than a color that shrinks the elevation of personal ego and exalts the connection to the source? If you have twins or siblings who have trouble distinguishing their individual personas, you might eliminate or reduce the orange in their environment.

Orange May Be Appropriate

- to foster cooperation
- to remove feelings of isolation
- where families are blended

Orange May Be Inappropriate

- for twins or siblings close in age

- to foster independence
- for a child who is suffering separation anxiety
- for a child with a highly successful sibling

Arielle's early language development did not impress her parents, for they expected their offsprings to be outstanding. Arielle was the only boisterous, physically active child in a family of serious, quiet, intellectual people. When she was six years old, this chatty, friendly child suddenly became morose. It was my observation that she never received the same attention as the older siblings. When I visited her room and saw the newly installed wallpaper of giant orange pansies in her room, I recommended a change. I asked her parents to fashion screens of fabric stretched over six-foot dowels. I told them to simply sew hems and push the dowels through. Then hang one or two screens from ceiling hooks to hide the pansy border from Arielle's view when lying in bed. I asked them to select a print that contained the colors yellow and red, which more closely represented Arielle's innate personality. This optimistic, active child who obviously had much to offer would be spurred to be herself when surrounded by yellow and red.

As it was in this case, it is not always easy to remove things that have just been installed. It may be better to alter a space in a way that is inexpensive and doesn't destroy what exists until you see that a permanent change is justified by the positive modification of a child's behavior.

Simple, Inexpensive Ways to Alter Color

- Hem fabric over a dowel and mount the hanging across a window, from the ceiling, or on the wall.
- Use felt or fabric of a similar weight as a washable area rug.
- Hang an umbrella upside down from the ceiling to test a new design motif.
- Use blankets, sarongs, or ethnic fabrics as bedspreads.
- Glue gift-wrapping paper on inexpensive window shades or over a mirror.
- Mount a T-shirt with appropriate designs on the wall using pushpins.
- Cascade ribbons vertically from the tops of curtains to change a plain fabric into a striped one.

Purple

An aura of mysticism surrounds the color purple. First of all, purple is not just a mixture of blue and red, but a mixture of magenta with blue. Over the course of Western history, purple has commonly been associated with power and spirituality. Purple is also used for Catholic clergy's robes and accessories for certain occasions and for the coverings of sacred books lodged in synagogues.

Purple promotes daydreaming and fantasizing. When absorbed in spinning fantasies in the mind, a child may appear to have fewer verbal skills than is actually the case. It may be compared to eating dinner at home before going out to a restaurant: you appear to have a small appetite when in truth you were thoroughly satisfied beforehand.

Children who have to spend a great deal of their childhood without the companionship of other children may benefit from having purple in their spaces. Purple brings an inner peace and tranquility to an area. Like blue it turns the mind inward, but unlike blue it encourages mental fantasy and playful reveries. Purple does not prompt the serious or self-focusing attention that blue does.

Purple May Be Appropriate

- for a child undergoing difficulties
- to nurture daydreaming
- to lessen physical pain
- to heighten the pleasure of time spent alone

Purple May Be Inappropriate

- for a child excessively focused on negativity
- for a child who is oversensitive when interacting with others
- if a child is unreasonably unwilling to participate in common housekeeping tasks

Lonnie was born with multiple sclerosis and struggled appropriately with the realities of the disease. To heighten his connection with a quiet inner world, I suggested that his parents use lavender and purple with dashes of blue and orange as the color scheme in his room. This combination elevates self-esteem and fusion with reality and encourages day-dreaming. These colors were selected to assist him with establishing a tranquil inner life.

Although only seven, Tasha's concerns and interests were uncommonly adult. Her mother worried about her excessive concern when she heard someone was sick. That and a passion for the TV program "Touched by an Angel," which provided weekly scenarios of dreaded circumstances miraculously interceded in by someone acting angel-like, led us to want to refocus this child's attention. I was not surprised to learn that Tasha had selected purple as her bedroom's color two years before. She had not chosen a light lavender, but a deep resinous, midnight-toned purple. The depth of hue and the color magnified her focus on life-and-death questions, for as you have learned, purple is the color of the unseen world.

Since Tasha was very young she had collected colored rubber balls dispensed at supermarkets and other chain stores; she loved looking at them. I suggested that we use her collection to change her room's colors. We sliced all of the balls in half and mounted them on twelve-inch-square pieces of heavy cardboard or wood. We strung wire across the backs and hung the entire thing on the diagonal. I recommended that they be mounted on a wall frequently viewed, such as the wall across from the door or the one across from the head of the bed. The variety of colors would lighten the room, the three-dimensional round objects would draw her eye away from the deeper wall color, and the diagonal overall shape would energize and ignite her mental processes toward more mirthful subjects.

Brown

Parents seldom choose earth colors to decorate children's rooms. Perhaps browns, taupes, tans, and terra-cottas seem dispirited and solemn in comparison to childhood's exuberance. But earth colors tie us to reality and whisper the messages of stability, security, and comfort. Consider how children love to play in the mud and adore feeling, rolling around on, and sitting on the earth. Children can easily use their bodies and are generally less fearful or hesitant to do so than adults. Maybe that means they have less need to be surrounded by a color that exudes what they themselves do perfectly well. Lying, sitting, and standing seem almost interchangeable, and the transition from one position to another seems effortless.

Therefore the color brown and its message of stability might be antithetical to a great deal of childhood's experiences.

Brown is a color lacking the zip that communicates activity and movement. For a nonphysical child or one with motor skills compromised by illness or an accident, the colors of the earth can help him or her feel less anxious about performing at the same level of speed and agility as other children.

Dark colors without high contrast can be frustrating for children whose eyesight is less than perfect (this does not apply to brown only). Scary shadows and unclear images fuel apprehension. If you do use dark colors in a child's space, make sure you add a great deal of illumination around them.

Brown May Be Appropriate

- to provide additional feelings of security and safety
- to stabilize
- for children with motor disabilities

Brown May Be Inappropriate

- for a quiet and shy child
- when a child's room faces north or is not sunny
- when the room's other furnishings are dark
- when a child lacks initiative

Black

Underused and underrated, black is a great color to use in children's spaces when contrasted with other colors. Fully saturated colors or primary colors are the ones infants can see easily. As the world becomes clearer and more intelligible, children are able to discern subtleties with greater ease. In the same way dim light obscures perception, the color black appears to lack light or is perceived as a hole.

It is not unusual for a child to fear the dark. The lack of definition, coupled with many children's lack of confidence about possibilities or knowledge of the surrounding world, creates an uncertain environment. Therefore, use black in conjunction with bright or light colors. For example, use a black satin pillowcase for a budding actor or actress or a black insert in a rug to promote focus to a particular area of a room.

Black commands instant attention in part because the eye seeks to define what is present. Black is experienced as a hole, and the eye naturally looks for danger or to uncover what is possible. Just like it feels impossible to lean over a quiet body of water and not try to see the bottom, seeing black makes us want to peer through it.

Black May Be Appropriate

- for an infant's room, to sharpen contrast between objects
- to organize areas in a room
- to reduce glare
- to add mystery

Black May Be Inappropriate

- when it obscures clear cognition of space
- when it is not contrasted with other colors
- when a child is fearful of the dark
- when its shape is amorphous and can be perceived as a shadow at night

White

White is the opposite of black because it reflects rather than absorbs all colors. White releases a glare and promotes alertness. It is harder to relax when there are great expanses of white in a room. Like a desert's illumination by an uncompromising sun, white does not relax the spirit.

White and all reflective surfaces spark the mind. In some ways white can be used as a distraction, for it diminishes the specificity of a view. Moreover, it is harder to feel stymied and downtrodden in a white space, unless circumstances dictate such an emotional reaction, as in a hospital. In the darkest of nights, white can give a room an air of lightness. A white surface across from a child's bed can sometimes counter nighttime fears.

Because white activates thinking, a child who worries too much, talks too much, or indulges in an activity with too much intensity and frequency can be overstimulated by too much white.

White May Be Appropriate

- for a child whose eyesight is poor
- when alertness is desired
- to enhance optimism
- to counteract the fear of darkness

White May Be Inappropriate

- for a child who cannot stop talking
- for a child who worries
- for a child with difficulty relating to other children
- for a child who requires too much adult attention

I used to frequent a home, not in a professional capacity but as a guest, so the following feng shui cure never had the opportunity to be tested. Carrie was a show-off. She worked hard at trying to snatch attention away from others. The family's living room was white and in that setting people stood out sharply because the background did not require attention. It was very hard for anyone to string two sentences together when Carrie was in the room because of her constant insistence on turning everyone's focus on herself. It was as if she wanted to be on stage and have everyone else in the audience, silently listening to her.

One time, however, I walked into her bedroom while she was playing with two cousins. Her bedroom was furnished with a profusion of subdued prints and colors. The light blues and pinks chosen were perfect for her personality, as were the checks and flower prints, for they diffused her as the center of attention. I couldn't believe it—she was almost passive, certainly egalitarian, in interacting with these two children and my presence was barely noticed beyond a casual look. Now maybe it was the fact that she was in her room, or maybe is was the fact that the all-white living room brought out the show-off in her, I don't know. But I do know that people stand out against white and that white can be a poor backdrop in a gathering setting if a child tends to need to be the center of attention.

Had I been asked, I would have suggested draping a variety of different quiet throws over the sofa and rearranging some of the artwork so the room would have more color and texture, lessening the sharp focus the décor had on those who occupied it.

Using Colors

It's one thing to select a color, but deciding how much to use, where to apply it, and how long to keep it in a given space are questions that need to be addressed.

Amount

Most children need a mixture of colors in their surroundings. To select the dominant color, match your child's personality needs with a color's characteristics. What color brings the most benefits to your child? Other needs will be satisfied by lesser amounts of secondary colors. There are no two colors that cannot work together, so don't worry about aesthetics. In nature all colors look good side by side.

Only in extreme cases will it be advantageous to select only one color. Think about creating such an extreme atmosphere only if your child requires the utmost relief of a single negative characteristic.

Place

Placement of colors is equal in importance to what the colors are. There are several important places to consider in any room. They are (in this order) the wall seen directly ahead when entering a room, the areas seen from the places of frequent activity (the bed, a game table, or the floor), and other play surfaces. Of course, if your child spends an inordinate amount of time in a particular part of a room, that location is the most important. The color that needs to be dominant should have extensive coverage in at least one of these areas.

Change

Finally, it is fun to consider ways to create a room that can easily accommodate change as your child matures. Since the stages of childhood move rather quickly, it is important to create a space that permits flexibility so that when your child's space needs a change, little money or effort is required to make the alterations. You want to avoid a situation in which a teenager is living in the room geared for a seven year old or a preschooler is stuck with the designs of infancy.

Let your imagination be your guide. I find that creative storefront display windows can spark some terrific ideas. Most important, when it's age appropriate, let your child be involved with this process.

Color and the Stages of Early Childhood

The rest of this chapter is devoted to examining the specific stages of early childhood in light of the generic use of color. This information bundled with the specific characteristics of your child will help you create great spaces for your child.

The Me, Myself, and I Stage (Birth to Eighteen Months)

During the first eighteen months of life a child is engrossed in learning to identify and define objects in the physical world. Consequently, shapes of edges and outlines are important. The more vivid and clear a boundary is, the easier it is to ascertain a shape. An infant perceives objects that are sharply contrasted with their background. As a child's age ascends to this stage's limits, he or she will have less difficulty identifying the perimeter of complex forms. The younger the child, the more distinctly delineated edges should be in his or her environment.

Pale colors without high contrast keep the world fuzzy and amorphous. Therefore, fully saturated colors are desirable. This simply means using a color's primary value with nothing that lightens or mutes its impact. The use of primary colors in a field of contrasting color makes it easier to assess a given shape.

According to Faber Birren in his book, *The Power of Color*, the **color combinations easiest to discern** by the human eye are, in descending order, as follows:

yellow on black
black on yellow
green on white
red on white

blue on white
white on blue
black on white

Solid colors plainly define objects. But patterns may also be appropriate. When deciding on colors for an infant's space, take the following into consideration:

Solids are the clearest.
Stripes define length.
Circles rivet attention.
Diamond shapes encourage tracking
    a pattern.
Squares focus attention.

In general large shapes with distinctly defined edges are clearer, as they beckon the eye to focus more than small patterns do.

Large, distinct shapes are best for infants' spaces.

The Magician Stage (Eighteen Months to Three Years)

The Magician is poised in a world between the undifferentiated self and the emergence of a self as separate. The Magician stage is characterized by the child's belief that he or she is the center of the universe. Only over time do children in this stage learn to appreciate that the world exists separately and apart from their control. (The Magician passes to the On the Road to Reason stage when his or her ego is clearly separate.)

Redundancy of color in locations that support similar activities can help the Magician make the connection from room to room. For example, if you keep your child's toys in baskets, choose one color for toy baskets no matter which room the basket is in. If you have several children and only one is in the Magician stage, keep just the Magician's toys in like-colored baskets throughout the home. The choices of colors can solidify a Magician's sense of place, and repetition of a hue can be comforting. As children learn to comprehend the nature of self, their world needs to feel extra secure. Repetition provides this comfort level.

Follow these guidelines when deciding on colors for a Magician's space:

Repeat colors in related activity centers.
Pay attention to colors within view in activity centers.
Copy a color used in a family's gathering space in a child's bedroom.

The On the Road to Reason Stage (Three to Six Years)

Bear in mind that during this stage the emergence of the self in relationship to the surrounding environment is taking place. How is the natural environment supported in your child's space? Too often parents fill a child's room with colors conceived more by commercial dyes than by objects in nature. At this stage of development, play spaces replicating the variety and hue of the outdoors are best.

Skew light as it is in nature by filtering it. Pierced screens or garlands of cutouts strung across windows form dancing shapes on nearby surfaces. Like nature, variety is inherently more nurturing than austerity, even when light is used as a palette. A room with overwhelming colors can thwart inventiveness. A variety of moderately saturated colors that relate to nature best support children during this stage of development.

Pierced materials in front of light sources support changing patterns on all colored surfaces.

In all areas of a home, the palette should be aligned enough with nature to remove the walls from your home and have the rooms look as if they belonged in the setting. If a home feels natural in its geographical setting, then the palette used reinforces the relationship of the person with place. If you ever visited transplanted Northerners in Florida who have retained their dark furnishings and color schemes after they moved, then you have experienced a setting being out of sync with its landscape.

Finally, don't worry about if your child's room looks good enough for the pages of a glossy home decorating magazine. What is most important is to honor a child's essential nature by furnishing with colors that enhance his or her strengths. Choosing colors to complement a child's personality will bestow upon the child gifts far greater than good design.

If a child experiences a trauma, the setting's colors may trigger strong reactions. I remember the day my parents moved me away from my childhood neighborhood, where I grew up with many of my close relatives. Our two-family house sheltered cousins who were almost like siblings to me. Leaving the familiar to cross into unknown territory remains indelibly associated in my mind with a dark blue car. Our family vehicle was stuffed to the roof with necessities that could not be trusted to the moving van. My world was absconding in the jaws of a deep blue steel container, and I was miserable. The pain of separation is forever associated with this memory. In my twenty-five years of being a car owner, I have never chosen, wanted, longed for, or bought a blue car, or selected upholstery in any shade or hue of blue. An accident? I don't think so.

8

Space to Move

Life's journey begins with the egg traveling from the ovary to the uterus and then sperm swimming toward the egg. Life is sparked on its inevitable path when the egg divides. Thus movement is, in some way, the initial expression of life.

Many automatic responses are associated with movement. Your eyes widen when you're startled, and your mouth curls upward when you're happy and when you're fearful. These are common ones. But did you realize that your nose instinctively curls upward when you encounter an unpleasant smell? Moving various body parts is an intrinsic reaction to many experiences.

An Environment of Texture, Movement, and Space to Move In

Stillness evokes concern in parents. A motionless child will likely be questioned about whether he or she is feeling well or is unhappy, mad, or sad. On the other hand, an active infant who is crawling, rolling, smiling, and looking around is a comfort to parents. Much has been written about touch-deprived and constrained children, mostly found in institutional settings. If left unattended for a period of time, these children become still and unresponsive.

Texture

In feng shui we can extrapolate that the experience of textures and their variety can add measurably to a child's inclination for investigation and, hence, activity levels. Textural variety encourages exploration.

Range of Textures

TEXTURE	ITEM
Stimulating to touch	With ridges, like corduroy
	With smooth pile, like velvet
	With hand-spun threads
	With uneven pile surfaces, like terry cloth
Cool to the touch	Silky
	Satiny
	Natural fiber with open weave
Warm to the touch	Densely woven fabrics
	Wool
	Padded, like a quilt
	Heated, like a hot water bottle wrapped in a towel
Dry	Blocks
	Books
	Toys without movement
	Oven mitts
Wet	Water toys for baths
	Sponges
	Paintbrushes, for paint or use with water
	Wet sand
	Deep bowls used for small water toys

Movement

The human eye is captivated by anything that moves. This instinctive attraction is a protective biological response for survival. In our species' early days it was crucial to discern if predators were present. Movement signaled the tiger whose panting agitated the leaves nearby and the snake whose slithering parted the grass. Humans developed innate abilities to notice movement because it might signal the need for a quick response. A child's room without the benefit of objects that move independently is a dull environment, one that does not stimulate or engage the child. Include some of these items that move naturally in your child's space:

Responsive to Air Movement

mobiles near a window or an entrance door
ribbons attached to ceiling fans
lightweight curtains
lightweight bamboo, bells, or sticks hung on a closet or entrance
    door (an added advantage is sound)

Responsive to Use

cushions or pillows that change shape with use or touch
beanbags
wheels
balls, all shapes and sizes
balloons
feathers

Space to Move In

Be cognizant of your child's need to negotiate through space. While we accept the fact that children will explore and move through a space, we often don't consider how to encourage a variety of movements. Provide options in your home that afford your child the experience of moving freely in space and assuming different postures.

Moving Freely in Space

Stand at the entrance to the rooms frequented by your child to see how many pathways there are for her to proceed without being blocked. Remember children can and will squeeze through spaces that adults cannot. For example, if a side table is not directly up against a chair, a child may be able to squeeze through the space between the table and the chair.

Remove any wires and reposition edges of area carpets that may entangle a child trying to squeeze through a tiny space where adults could never tread. If you cannot walk a minimum of three steps in a child's bedroom or three to four steps in the main gathering space without having to stop, then there is not enough room for a child to feel a sense of freedom. Moreover, there should be at least two different pathways through a room to provide adequate options for movement. Reposition tables or furniture if necessary.

Assuming Different Body Postures

A child's body is more flexible than most adults'. When physical limitations are not imposed, a young child will walk, leap, roll, topple, skip, hop, and run with ease. Movement is as natural in early childhood as water flowing down a hill.

In comparison with children, adults use space rather simply. We walk through it, sit, or lie down. Most of us can't remember the last time we used our bed as a trampoline, the couch pillows as hurdles for leaping over, or the floor as a playing field. Examine the spaces your child uses vertically. Think of a child's space as a large ladder and see how many rungs there are and how easily a child might negotiate the various levels. If only floor, seating, and bed planes are available, consider adding more levels.

Outdoor-Type Movement Indoors

A major objective in creating a space for your child is to provide opportunities for outdoor-type movement indoors. Remember: the more opportunity for diversity of experience, the closer in complexity indoor space is to outdoor spaces. Since human anatomy was designed to negotiate and survive an outdoor environment, it is reasonable to consider the movement options offered in nature and replicate them indoors. Here's a comparison list that gives you some depth of movement options to consider:

Replicating Outdoor Opportunities for Movement

LEVELS OF SPACE	THEIR OUTDOOR EQUIVALENT
Penetrating spaces at ground level	Digging holes, burying oneself in sand, exploring caves
Negotiating a variety of levels	Running or rolling down a hill
Sitting just above ground level	Sitting on a felled log, on a stone, or in a streambed
Climbing higher than knee level	Scaling low tree branches or piles of stones
Walking on uneven surfaces	Balancing on a log over a stream
Scaling heights	Climbing a tree or hill

Penetrating Spaces at Ground Level and Crawling Underneath Things

No, it is not necessary to dig up floorboards or drill holes in the floor to re-create nature in your home. I know one set of parents who built a box with a sliding door. With the door closed the box was used as a child's seat just above ground level, but when the top was pushed to the side, the box changed into a cavern for their child to descend into. As it turned out, the box became their child's favorite place to leaf through books. Think of the satisfying feeling of snugly reading with a flashlight hidden by the bed covers. Children love cavernous places to pursue quiet activities.

A stool with legs, crawl-through tubing, and of course a skirted table can provide experiences of discovery and intrigue.

If carpentry is not your cup of tea, create the same kind of experience by building a "cave" out of foam rubber rectangles covered in pillowcases and topped with a translucent sheet. Or use a stool or skirted table.

Negotiating a Variety of Levels

Consider the difference between playing in a placid pool of water and swimming in the ocean. While both can be refreshing, the stimulation of waves makes frolicking in the ocean exhilarating. In providing your child with spaces to practice negotiating a variety of levels, you certainly don't want *only* high-energy areas, but a few in selected areas. Find a space where your child's romping doesn't pose a threat. Be sure there are no sharp edges, breakable treasures, or electrical wires or outlets. Then consider making a few lumpy additions to the floor. Place pillows under blankets, or toss rolled-up blankets near walls. Be sure to create a place your child can reach down to. Hanging upside down is fun for children. Sofas, chairs, or a raised niche can be used as a platform so that children can hang like opossums.

You can also use other household objects, like step aerobic equipment, to create variety at ground level. Step platforms can be stacked up to form a sturdy plateau, as can floor pillows and large oven pans. Consider too the additional possibilities these items afford. The step platform can become a stage on which to set up toys; the pillows, walls for a fort; and the oven pan, a container for small toys.

Climbing Higher than Knee Level

With feet off the ground, but not so high as to cause parental trepidation, children can be in a vantage point that bestows a sense of adventure without risk. A cardboard box taped closed will suit these requirements, as will any plank stretched across two chair seats. Stools are very useful. Not only are they small and transportable, but they also easily convert into a ready-made tunnel under which to crawl. Building supply stores stock sonar tubing used as forms for pouring concrete. With a small section affixed to the floor, they provide a smooth, rounded surface to crawl over and a dark cavelike space to wriggle through.

Scaling Heights

Sometimes I have to stand on my kitchen counter to retrieve an item from the top shelf of the cabinets. The perspective of looking down is both exhilarating and novel. Children delight in a bird's-eye view. In every one of my own homes I created a loft area over a main gathering space. Used as an extra sleeping space or a children's play area, this raised level is reached by a ladder that swings down from its underside and is a favorite space for visiting children.

A simple old-fashioned swing seat, hoops on ropes hanging from the ceiling, a pedestal affixed to the floor, or a short length of eighteen-inch-wide shelving can all be used to create spaces to climb up to.

Boundaries

Bouncing on sofas and hanging from curtain pulls or cords may be commendable from a developmental standpoint but are hard to tolerate unless appropriate spaces are created to satisfy the basic need of children to move. Moreover, adults are often confounded by the unpredictability of children's movements, and the way to mitigate adult irritation is create appropriate boundaries in the home.

Boundaries permit access to diverse territories. Consider how seductive a door to an unexplored area can be because of the excitement of discovering what is hidden behind it. After exploring, a child has clear, secure knowledge of expected behavior. Even in the open layout plan of many early childhood centers, a variety of floor coverings and placement of furnishings are provided to create boundaries. In your child's space, remember to have some things hidden out of sight. Opportunities for discovery are so beneficial to the feeling of mastery in early childhood. A well-planned child's space could have many of these boundary features:

curtains
area carpets
backs of furniture
screens
stacked boxes
strung ropes

Boundaries help children manifest self-control, because when there are clear, concise expectations, it is easier to react appropriately. Only when there are not enough options for children to test the limits of their physical abilities will they resort to less acceptable alternatives.

Children need to be able to bounce off things, charge, climb, move with eyes closed, tumble, leap, and wriggle to fully express themselves in space. Provide opportunities for enough diversity of movement to meet these needs. Moving though space teaches children mastery, which increases their self-confidence.

PART II
Children's Section

9

Fairy Schway

Growing a Room

T his chapter is designed to show you how to create a partnership between you and your child through the story about Fairy Schway.

In order to do so, you must explain new concepts and vocabulary to your child that will be used when shaping his or her room. When your child is approximately three years of age, the story of Fairy Schway and feng shui can genuinely assist you in cocreating an environment that will be intrinsically more meaningful for your child. Read the entire story to your child, perhaps several times over a few weeks.

Parents, stretch yourselves and come aboard!
Suspend disbelief; you won't be bored.
Reaching shores not imagined as true,
Shrink not from the strange or even new.
Suspending disbelief to things elusive
Can ultimately prove most conclusive.
Here's knowledge that for now is veiled.
With a child on your lap, begin reading this tale!

Growing a Room

Last night in my mind I had a dream
That in my window flew a fairy queen.
"Who are you?" I asked, surprised
'Cause magic and mystery usually pass me by.

"Fairy Schway," was her reply,
And into my room she plopped from the sky.
"I'm here to teach you that you never have to roam,
For all things you need are here at home!
I'll help your bedroom become a space for you
To grow healthier, happier, and smarter too."

With that she waved her magic wand
And all the things in my room were gone.

"We'll place them back when a spot is found
But for now we'll keep them outside, on the ground.
Before I bring them back indoors
I'll turn my knowledge into yours."

Then before me like a zooming car
Fairy Schway flew out, among the stars,
Hauling colorful, fluttering kites with words
With strange names like exotic birds:
The *Tao*, *yin* and *yang*, and of course the *chi*.
"You will learn what these mean," she promised me.

Yin and yang

Chi

"The *Tao* is merely the natural way
We're supposed to live, work, and play.
On just one part we can't rely
Or live without outside, inside.

"If you bring back all the things that are alive
Like pets and plants and bugs that hide
Even photographs of animals or a meadow will do,
Then the Tao will be inside with you."

Oh good, I have that photo still
Of when we visited Uncle Bill,
His farm with cows and pigs and goats
And Mom and me in winter coats.

I also have a potato growing
With three big leaves already showing.
How about my stuffed animals in my red toy bin?
Will bringing them back move the outside in?

With much amazement as I sat
My room just started growing back.
The trick of having the Tao, it seems,
Is having the outside inside with me.
Returned to my room was some of my favorite stuff.
"Fairly Schway," I bellowed, "this isn't tough!"

"The next are words for two extremes
Like playing for real or in a dream.
Yin and *yang* are their given names,
And they are opposites, which are the same,
Like skipping or running are ways to race
And grinning or frowning are two kinds of face.

"Like sugar is sweet and salt is sharp
And morning is light while night is dark.
Each opposite cannot exist alone
Just like a voice without a tone."

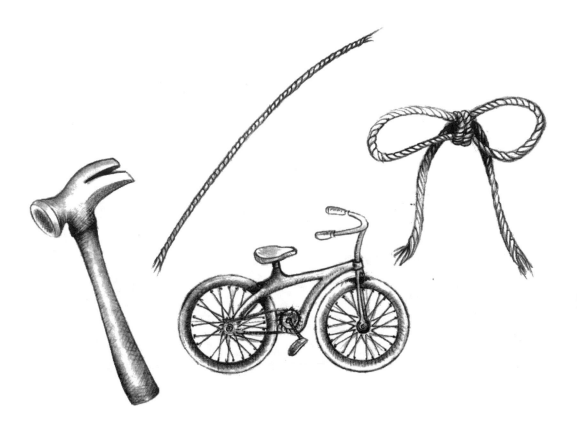

"I got it," I bellowed, and jumped up with joy!
"Like a hammer is a tool, and a bike is a toy!
Like a string can be straight or bent in a loop
Or I can jump up or crouch down in a stoop."

Big and little, fast and slow
Up and down, rip apart or sew.
Opposites when used together
Can make each extreme a little better.

When you're cold, turn on the heat,
And if you're tired, go to sleep.

Then all the things that helped me sleep
Flew back inside in a giant heap
Together with my action toys,
Like dolls and bikes and other joys.
"Play needs rest as you can see
And opposites are meant to be!"

"Will we be finished this very night?
'Cause my parents get up before it's light."

"Of course we will," said Fairy Schway.
"For chi will help us pave the way.
Good chi is spunk and energy
And all things that make you shout 'Yippee.'
Chi is all things heard, smelled, seen, and touched.
Chi helps us discover that the world has so much.

"Some chi can make us feel real small.
Some chi can block a rolling ball.
Some chi smells are nice and some smell bad.
Some chi makes us happy and some makes us mad.
Some chi can burn our clothes or skin.
And ice cream's chi can double our chin."

Rug, chair, and bed all returned.
"Wow!" I thought of all I'd learned.

Left on the lawn were things that could
Hamper me from being good.
"That sharp arrow is a bad kind of chi
For it could harm one of my friends or me!"

My room was back a little changed
Though nothing was new or even strange,
Just arranged with my new friends three:
The Tao, ying and yang, the chi, and *me!*

Then Fairy Schway leaped up into the night
Sprinkling stardust on me before she took flight.
"There is much more for you to learn.
So it is written I shall return.

"I will think of you as Little Chi.
It's a secret name between you and me.

"For now just remember your new friends three:
The Tao, yin and yang, and good and bad chi."

Then she kissed my cheek and stepped into the sky

"Good night, Little Chi, good night, not good-bye!"

10

The Children's Test

This test is designed to help you determine your child's leanings regarding the basic feng shui principles of the five elements and yin and yang, as well as reinforce his or her understanding of the feng shui principles of chi and the Tao.

The test is divided into several sections with answers and analysis at the end of each section. If you have more than one child at home, be sure to test each child separately. This test is appropriate for children who can identify and distinguish animals and colors, have an understanding of rudimentary social situations, and have had reasonably diverse life experiences. A child approaching the On the Road to Reason stage should be able to complete this test. Its results will provide meaningful materials for parents.

In order to know how to manipulate your child's environment, it is important to understand the overall way he or she interfaces with reality. Access your child's personality first through observation and then administer the Children's Test to verify your evaluation.

The Five Elements

Have your child respond to the following drawings that will reveal his or her elemental leanings. Ask your child the questions corresponding to each picture. The answers are likely to divulge a child's inclination toward an elemental personality category.

1. Which of these animals is your favorite?

2. Which of these animals is your least favorite?

The giraffe represents wood; the octopus, metal; the bird, fire; the elephant, earth; and the fish, water. It is likely that your child's favorite animal is the elemental characteristic most expressed in his or her personality. His or her least favorite animal is least expressed in his or her personality.

Chi

Use this section for exposing your child to good and bad chi. Describe each scene with your child, reviewing whether it represents good or bad chi.

3. Examples of Good and Bad Chi

Good Chi

Expressing yourself through music and dance

Bad Chi

Hurting another person

GOOD CHI

Reading a book

BAD CHI

Loud noises

Jumping rope or other physical activity

Not paying attention to your surroundings

When your child can tell which scenes represent good chi, he or she has a good understanding of the principle.

Yin and Yang

The questions in this section have to do with yin and yang. Once you have ascertained your child's yin or yang tendencies, you can determine in what atmosphere he or she would feel most comfortable.

Children's personalities may lean toward either yin or yang, although, on the whole, childhood is a yang state. Because children are by nature exuberant and seem to be literally bursting with energy, it is important to ascertain the basic temperament of your children to determine whether you need to encourage yin or yang aspects in the spaces they inhabit.

Use question 4 for teaching your child what conditions are yin and what are yang. Read each list item to your child, reviewing whether it is yin or yang.

4.   Examples of Yin and Yang

Yin	Yang
small	big
sweet	sour
dark	light
cold	hot
curvy	straight
quiet	noisy
thin	fat

closed	open
resting	active
moon	sun
flat land	mountains
quiet water	waves
winter	summer

When your child can tell which conditions are yin and which are yang, he or she has a good understanding of the principle.

It is likely that you have a good idea if your child's personality is yin or yang. What you may not know is if his or her internal spirit or emotional self is closely aligned with what is shown externally. This test is designed to reveal the dimension and reach that your child feels within the context of yin and yang. In other words, a normally outgoing child may in fact need or feel comfortable with a quieter yin atmosphere. To the extent that your assessment of your child is consistent with his or her choices on this test of yin and yang, you can ascertain whether to counteract or support your child's natural tendencies.

5. On which side of the picture would you like to live?

Yin—the night scene; yang—the day scene

For questions 6 through 17, show your child the pictures and ask the questions. Answers appear at the end of this chapter.

6. WHICH PART OF THE BALL DO YOU LIKE?

the part with stripes

the part with circles

7. WHICH BOX SHAPE DO YOU LIKE?

red triangular box

terra-cotta square box

green rectangular box

metallic circular box

deep blue irregular box

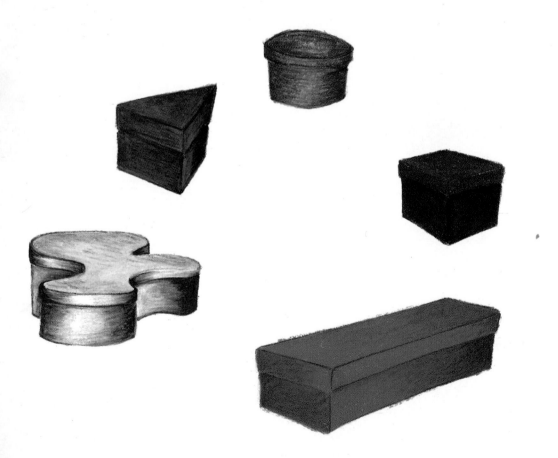

8. WHICH WOULD YOU LIKE TO LIVE IN?

red tent

tree house in a tall tree

blue houseboat on a
quiet pond

sailboat on wavy sea

igloo

square sod house

9. WHICH BLOCK DO YOU LIKE?

the square, dark-colored one

the rectangular, brightly colored one

10. WHICH SHIRT WOULD YOU LIKE TO WEAR?

the striped one

the one with splotches

11. Who would you like to be?

bear eating honey

kangaroo jumping over a fire

12. HOW WOULD YOU LIKE TO TRAVEL?

in the rocket

on the back of the snail

13. WHICH PICTURE WOULD YOU WISH TO SEE THROUGH YOUR BEDROOM WINDOW?

a starry night

a trampoline in the sunshine

14. Which would you rather have in your bedroom?

a low dresser

a tall dresser

15. WHICH WOULD YOU RATHER EXPLORE?

the clouds

a cave

16. Which game would you rather be playing?

outside kicking a ball

inside playing a board game

17. WHOM WOULD YOU RATHER TALK WITH?

one friend

a group of friends

In the table below are the answers for questions 6 through 17 of the test, grouped by yin and yang.

Question Number	Yin	Yang
6.	The part with circles	The part with stripes
7.	Terra-cotta square box Metallic circular box Deep blue irregular box	Red triangular box Green rectangular box
8.	Blue houseboat on a quiet pond Igloo Square sod house	Red tent Tree house in a tall tree Sailboat on a wavy sea
9.	The square, dark-colored one	The rectangular, brightly colored one
10.	The flowered one	The striped one
11.	Bear eating honey	Kangaroo jumping over a fire
12.	On the back of the snail	In the rocket
13.	A starry night	A trampoline in the sunshine
14.	A low dresser	A tall dresser
15.	A cave	The clouds
16.	Inside playing a board game	Outside kicking a ball
17.	One friend	A group of friends

Your child may lean toward a picture because of its color or shape. If his or her explanation for choosing a particular figure includes color or shape, it may show a need for the element it represents. Conversely, if a figure is not chosen because of its color or shape, the opposite may be true. There is also a possibility that your child chooses certain figures because of their association with a favorite storybook or TV show. It is still likely, however, that you can uncover clues about your child's emotional leanings through this test.

PART III

Rooms and Special Considerations

11

Dining Areas

How many scenes from your childhood are attached to a family dining event? Do you have a children's table at family parties? Can you recall your mom agonizing about where to position guests at a dinner party? The dining table is the last bastion of family socialization. In a world filled with an overabundance of in-house entertainment choices, family togetherness and social communication is often limited to meals. Therefore, a table's seating has significant weight in structuring a child's self-perception and attitudes.

The Power Seat

Generally, it's inappropriate for a child to occupy the power seat at a family's dining table. Traditionally a central family member or guardian occupies the power seat, the chair against the power wall (see Chapter 6). That is not to say that you can't ever put a child in the power seat, but it is imperative to consider the effect doing so may have on the family as a whole and on each individual member.

The power wall is across from the most frequently used entrance. The pyramid school of feng shui locates the entrance of any space at the most frequently used threshold of the room. The actual main door or entrance may or may not be the one used most frequently. For example, an eat-in kitchen's most frequently used entrance may be through the main part of the kitchen or an adjoining room. The architectural entrance is not always the main entrance.

A curtainless window behind a power seat compromises the position's power, especially if the window is facing west or a busy street. In this case, the glare of either the setting sun or the headlights of a passing car will be distracting. Thus, a power wall with a window open to an engaging or diverting view compromises the power invested in the person who sits with his or her back to that position.

Many years ago, I had clients who couldn't understand why their two year old turned into a dictator during mealtimes. They told me that their child's behavior was nothing out of the ordinary at other times, so I became suspicious of the seating pattern at the dining table.

It was a classic. The family's dining room was at the end of a fairly long living room. The child sat at the long side of the rectangular table with his back to a windowless wall in what I call the power position.

Like royalty on a throne, my clients' child had the full view of the room, and his parents viewed him against a solid wall with no windows or openings to distract their attention when facing him. The kitchen entrance was on the child's left, which is the side that a person is least likely to turn toward, and his father was on his right. To make matters worse, his parents sat across from each other at the ends of the long table. The distance was too far away for intimacy and even made general social exchanges difficult because it was necessary for them to raise their voices to be heard. Our "little emperor" was the fulcrum for all attention and activity. He soon caught on and used his dominant position to hand down edicts befitting a monarch.

Having the following items on the power wall can compromise the power seat. These will diffuse a child's power over others at the table.

How to Detract Power from a Power Seat

window
outside scene with movement
clock with moving parts
painting with a depth view
entrance to another room

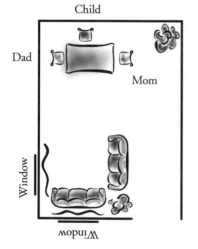

A classic power seat is facing the most frequently used entrance backed by an unbroken wall.

Messages on the Walls

Walls give us an opportunity to place appropriate messages. Use wall space to hang pictures or mementos that are appropriate for the person who faces them. As I have pointed out, the dining experience is a last bastion for family camaraderie where interruptions from the outside are frequently banned. It is often the only time a family will not answer the telephone and the TV is turned off. Therefore, what is seen has a greater influence on a child than in a room with frequent distractions.

We are biologically programmed to check out edges of a space. It is in our nature to instantly seek the farthest point in any space in order to determine if we are safe. Not long ago I was visiting a household with two perfectly happy, well-adjusted children. Their mother complained to me that she couldn't understand why the boy was gaining so much weight. No one else in the family was heavy. She didn't keep junk foods at home and cooked a healthy dinner every night, yet her son would whine each evening if she had forgone a sweet dessert. After I discovered her son's seat at the dining table, I knew I had found one answer. Across from his seat hung a colorful print of children romping in what only can be described as a candy garden. This artist's imagination unleashed grass looking like licorice sticks, flowers with lollipop blooms, and pebbles shaped like chocolate candy. The distant hill looked like a snowball cookie, with its peak heavily sprinkled with coconut shreds. No wonder this child craved sweets! We moved the picture to a hallway and replaced it with a non-food-related print.

When deciding on wall hangings and room arrangements for dining areas, consider the following questions:

What is the farthest point in your dining area?
What painting hangs on that wall?
What is the artwork's message?
What subliminal messages are being evoked by the colors of the artwork?
If there is a window, does the view reflect the tone and style of how you wish your family to interact?

Height of each family member is a consideration when selecting seats around a table. If, for example, a dining area has two walls with windows, placing a tall member of the household against the window can screen the

> *Children take in all messages subconsciously, even the ones we don't lay claim to. I'm always struck by TV interviews with parents of a young person who has committed a violent crime with a gun. Inevitably, the parents declare that although they keep guns in the home, they have taught their children responsibility and correct handling of weapons. How can children see a locked gun cabinet every day of their lives and not end up being fascinated with it?*

distraction for a smaller member. The larger person simply obscures the smaller one's vision.

Carefully consider the items you place in the power area of a frequently used room for the message they send. The messages these items communicate to a child are significant and long lasting.

Arrangements Around a Table

Positioning is often key in how you feel about yourself in a situation. If you have a last name beginning with a letter close to the alphabet's end, then you might have experienced the effect of being at the end. If you were made to line up by height order, as I was in elementary school, and you happened to be one of the tallest, you know that being at the end of a line makes you feel out of the loop. In the same way, it matters who sits at the end of your family's dining table or who is singled out to sit alone on one side.

The person who sits to the right will be turned to and spoken to most frequently. Whoever sits on your child's right will naturally be the focus of his or her attention, the one with whom he or she engages in most conversation and interactions, unless there are mitigating factors.

If an older child ignores a younger one, you could seat the younger one to the right of the older one to encourage the older to engage the younger. And conversely, if one child seems to pick on another, the child receiving the insults could be placed to the left. Why, you may be thinking, do you not just separate them across a table? The fact is that in a study conducted by Edward T. Hall, considered by many to be the father of cultural anthropology, it was discovered that the illustrated seating patterns encouraged a higher level of conversation and interaction.

Moreover, Don Campbell, author of the popular book *The Mozart Effect*, further enlightens us about being spoken to in the right ear. His studies suggest that more emotional context is absorbed when you hear the information from the right side.

With an odd number of family members, be careful who is paired and who sits alone. Round tables are best when a family has an odd number of members.

Tammy is rearing triplets. Two are male identical twins, and the third is a fraternal female. If all were boys, the seating configuration at the dining table might not be so difficult. But there

(a) Two people sitting at right angles are likely to engage in a two-way conversation.

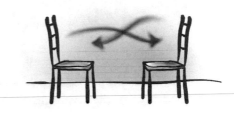

(b) Two people who are seated across from each other are in the position second most likely to foster interaction.

Considerations for Seating Family Members at a Dining Table

NEEDS	WHERE
To be secure	Between two others
To feel free	At the end of the row or at the head of the table
To be near the parents	At the right ear for emotions, at the left ear for listening to instructions (depending on what the child needs)
To establish independence	At the end of the table or with another member between
To lessen confrontational stress	Not directly across from another

(c) Two people will have fewer interchanges with one another when seated side by side.

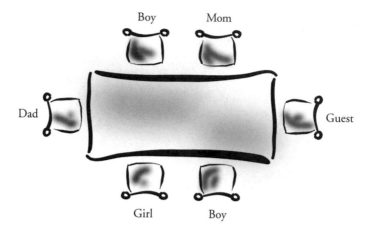

This dining arrangement avoids making the girl feel like the odd person out.

is a potential problem that the identical boys will feel very aligned because of their twinship and sex. The girl could potentially end up as the odd person out. The illustration shows what I suggested as a seating arrangement for this family.

Children often don't prefer staying still or seated. Having to sit down is often translated as chastisement, for children more typically like to move about. Selecting an appropriate place, one that advances their interests and minimizes conflicts, can make the difference between dining as a pleasurable family event or just another task to be completed.

12

Gathering Spaces

It is through play that a child acquires many of life's tools. Diane Ackerman, in her visionary book *Deep Play*, has defined play as "a state of unself-conscious engagement with our surroundings." This is exactly what a gathering space should promote.

The main gathering space should be a magnet for all family members. This space is not always architecturally appointed; families sometimes gather in kitchens, porches, dens, basements, or master bedrooms. It matters not what the name of the room is, just as long as it's the one to which members gravitate consistently.

In order to provide a well-equipped gathering space for your family, you must determine what categories of activity will take place there. Gathering space categories of activity include

Quiet zone
- sleep, nap, rest
- read
- listen

Play
- physical play
- dramatic play

Discovery
- manipulatives
- messy area
- eating surfaces
- arts and crafts
- science and nature

Group activities

You may want to be selective and not include all categories. The key is to select what is integral for your child and your whole family.

Quiet Zone

Many of us tend to think of children as noisy and active, so it is remarkable how many of their activities require a calm and understimulated atmosphere. Adults tend to relax on comfortable chairs, stretch out on sofas, and prop up their feet on almost anything, but children are more flexible. They engage in quiet activities quite happily snuggled on a blanket at the base of a chair, curled up under the legs of a table, or leaning on pillows in the crevice between two walls.

Sleeping

When my former husband Ben was a young child, he would conceal a safety pin from his mother while she read him his bedtime story. He surreptitiously pinned her skirt to his sheets in the hope that she would be trapped and unable to leave his side. Wanting to be close to someone when asleep is a biologically driven need for safety, security, and comfort. Consider the floor, a chair, a sofa, or even a table as an appropriate place for a child to rest, especially when you are nearby.

My friends from Maine have a lobster trap as a coffee table. This sturdy, rugged chest is sometimes used as a sleeping platform for their two year old, who loves to nap there on his blanket while resting his head on his father's outstretched leg. It is not at all necessary to create a separate and special place for resting.

Reading

Children need to be sheltered from distractions in order to read or listen with concentration. Such activities are best supported by a space not facing artwork with strong diagonal lines, stairs, flickering lights, or an area with shadows and stimulating colors such as red, bright yellow, or vivid orange.

Facilitate reading by resting a book on either a table or tray. Bed trays are good accessories, because they can be used on the floor, on a sofa, a table and, of course, a bed. They are portable, easy to clean, and collapsible.

Listening

Listening is often referred to as an art, and with feng shui's help, you can remove obstacles to listening.

I recently spoke with my six-year-old friend Barnaby, who was telling me how he liked his classes in computer and recess best when they were scheduled in that order. As a highly physical child he requires an opportunity to run about after being sedentary during computer class. For some children a room must have space for large motor activity as a balance to time spent listening.

To facilitate listening in a gathering room space, consider these factors:

- Position a child where he or she won't see red, orange, or green.
- Make sure a window, hallway, or doorway is not in view.
- It is easier for a child to listen to a person who is closer than eighteen inches from him or her. Moreover, it is easier for a child to pay attention to a person who is in thermal contact, that is, someone whose body heat the child can feel.
- Position a child so that he or she listens with his or her right ear.
- Earth elements' scents support focus and staying still. Fennel and lemon are two common choices.

Discovery

Childhood is a time of great exploration, when everything is a vehicle for discovery. A physical space must provide enough flexibility to allow a child to flourish in activities of discovery.

Manipulatives

Before a child's powers of mental abstraction are fully developed, the powers of tactile manipulation are dominant. Provide your child opportunities to turn over, take apart, form new, add, abridge, and revamp stuff.

When my cousin, Alan, was a child he loved to take apart alarm clocks or any other mechanism he could convince his parents he could reassemble. I suppose he was afraid his parents would change their minds if they observed springs, screws, and other innards sprawled around the floor, so he would take his booty and slip under the dining room table to dissect it. Since a hallway separated the dining room from the gathering room, he was often out of the loop, unable to listen in to the family conversations. Had his parents draped a cloth over the card table, which was part of the gathering space's décor, he could have had his privacy and auditory participation too. As a consequence of his separation, my cousin grew up with less enmeshment with his family.

Making Messes

Messy is not a parent's favorite word. Yet the truth is that children are not naturally tidy. Being messy is as normal as sneezing. Neatness is learned. Therefore some place in a home must be available for a bit of disorder and untidiness.

Activities that require cleanup don't have to be a parent's worst nightmare. Place cups of water and snippets of clay, flour, or any moldable material in large, shallow (one-half-inch high) plastic containers for your child to amuse herself with. Place the cups on trays with raised edges to prevent their leaching over to other areas. After the child's interest wanes, pick up the whole mess and take it to the cleanup area.

Contain children's messes inside a large cardboard box.

If you can be relaxed enough to have a bit of untidiness in your gathering space, here are a few suggested items that will help you contain the mess:

- a small outside pool used indoors, which you can just hose down outside to clean
- trays with lips
- a large, sealed cardboard box with a hole cut out for a door
- one-quarter-inch foam rubber mattress covering as a mat for the floor (can be rolled up with objects in it)
- oilcloth as a mat for the floor

Eating

Eating can be a discovery activity for children. You can indulge your child and still protect your furnishings. Before going to the expense of installing

My friend Sue tells a story about her mother, who used to rinse the dishes after a meal, then fill the sink with soapy water, and let her children "play," often with an (nonmotorized) egg beater in the water. When the children tired of this play, she washed off the dishes and her job was done. Sue used to give her own daughter baking soda to play with in the bathtub. The daughter spent time with measuring, pouring, and mixing activities while Sue read the newspaper on the bathroom floor, keeping an eye on her daughter. (Note: constant supervision of children in bathtubs is imperative, for a drowning child does not make a sound.)

easy-to-clean flooring surfaces, toss a cotton or canvas rug over the existing flooring, or put a cloth over existing surfaces. I used to toss a plastic tablecloth on the floor, for it was easy to scoop up and shake outside before wiping it off. A friend of mine with tile flooring uses a blower as a cleanup tool. She simply blows what has accumulated on the floor out the door.

Arts and Crafts

Baskets of yarn, buttons, safety scissors, glue, scraps of paper, glitter, magazines, and crayons can be stored attractively in a main room. Store materials used for experimenting in natural wicker hampers, under side tables, in decorative chests, or in any drawer. All kinds of materials can be used to while away hours constructively while the family is gathered together.

Science and Nature

Nothing is more delightful to most children than having the rich diversity of nature in which to wander. Indoor vignettes lack the transformative qualities of the natural world. A cardinal rule in pyramid feng shui is to always supply any setting with as many replications of the natural world as possible. Therefore, in a setting as important as the family's gathering room, a space devoted to a terrarium, a fishbowl, an ant colony—any item that houses something that moves, changes, and needs care—will bring in nature's wonders.

In my childhood, snacking in the living room was a great treat usually reserved for guests or for during the holiday seasons. I remember the elaborate preparations my mother made when bringing in the cups of steaming cocoa topped off with dollops of whipped cream. First she spread an oilcloth table covering over the carpeting. Afterward, she positioned my sister and me on the floor with our legs outstretched under a footed tray to receive the treat.

Play

I do not advocate removing art or table accessories to "childproof" a home, because children need to learn how to handle all kinds of objects. However, I do recommend having approximately three square feet of table surface and four square feet of floor space unencumbered. Children need some blank slate to pursue investigating whatever they are currently interested in. Feng shui's wisdom suggests that the center of a room feels most secure. Therefore, I suggest at least one unobstructed space be close to the center. This may mean exchanging a large coffee table for a smaller one to provide floor space between two couches or opening up a closed seating group.

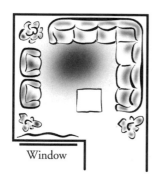

An unencumbered area near the center of a room provides a secure play space for a child.

Physical Play

Jumping, leaping, and tossing one's body around is normal in childhood. Large playthings such as riding toys, ropes to swing from, big blocks, and toys to chase after and jump on are the stuff of gross motor skills. A child thrives on moving through space unimpeded and unabashed.

What adult uses the back of a sofa as a cliff, a puppet stage, or a gym horse? Everything can serve children for a plethora of purposes. Look at your present room with an awakened sense of the possibilities. Consider whether your gathering space allows room for your children to perform the following gross motor skills:

skipping	acrobatics
running	balancing
playing tag	climbing
rolling	

If not, here are a few suggestions for creating areas for gross motor skills:

- Remove chairs around a table so its perimeter forms a path for running and skipping.
- Set up armless chairs in a row next to a wall to create a running or crawling track.
- Set a plank on two chairs to make a balance beam. (Put pillows underneath.)

Dramatic Play

Dramatic play affords children the opportunity to transform themselves in different personas. Even the crudest stage contains the fundamental poetry by which a child can imitate and replicate many real and imagined scenarios. From the chatter to no one in particular to elaborate group experiences, make-believe inhabits a deeply satisfying place in the psyche of growing up.

> *When my son Zachary was a small child, I referred to him as "Le Chef" when he would grace me with his presence while I was preparing dinner. As soon as he could focus enough to handle a knife and not randomly wave it around (at a little over two years old) I would let him prepare the dinner salad. He tore the mixed greens and used a pumpkin knife (usually sold around Halloween) to cut the tomatoes and cucumbers. His little face would light up with triumph when he boldly picked up the knife to begin his carving. I remember wondering at how little it took to delight him and increase his sense of mastery.*

Dramatic play includes

culinary creation	puppet play
housekeeping	dress-up
doll playing	fantasy themes

By ritualizing and exalting any mundane activity to one of play, you can empower your child. What housekeeping, child tending, clothes maintaining, or personal hygiene activities of your daily routine can be relegated to your child to provide him or her with the tools for dramatic play?

Group Activities

Naturally, a family's main room must serve the needs of all its members. It cannot be shaped only as a playground accommodating a child's needs. It must also be a place of rest and rejuvenation for adults. Consider how a fish tank, which brings nature indoors, can also serve as an adult's meditative focus. Consider how a flowing tablecloth concealing a child's hiding place or basket of toys can also add a variety of color and patterns appropriate to the season.

Make your family's gathering space a place where children can engage in activities side by side with adults. Reading, playing, conversing, and listening to music are the kinds of activities that all family members can participate in. When planning the layout of a gathering space, which must accommodate all family members, work within the following guidelines:

- Face children away from windows when attention or focus is required.
- Face the caretaker's seating toward the entrance of the room.
- Have some seating at right angles to encourage conversation.
- Make sure a lamp's pool of light falls over an entire area of play.
- Engage all senses. There should be a variety of things to smell, hear, see, and touch.
- Provide easy access to the seating area from the entrance.

In earlier times people lived mainly in one room. That room served the needs of not only all occupants but all activities. Since life was pri-

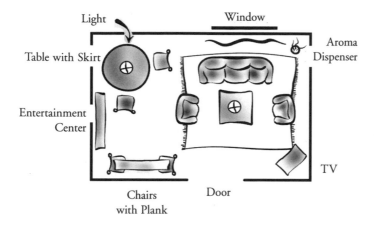

Plan a gathering space that serves all the family members.

marily focused on survival, activities of daily life were intricately enmeshed with that process. In contemporary America we enjoy a historically unparalleled time; subsisting is no longer fraught with peril, and life's major task is the pursuit of contentment. We are privileged to be able to focus on activities that are designed for personal growth and pleasure. Gathering spaces should invite individuals to explore their interests and release energies in creative pursuits. Don't let concern about material possessions preclude your family's using your gathering space to the fullest extent. Be unconcerned by others' scrutiny, for it is far better to elude measuring up to others' aesthetic standards than to compromise a child's unfettered exploration of himself or herself in the physical world.

13

Playrooms

P lay is interaction with the environment unencumbered by prescribed rules. Playing needs a responsive and transformable space, in which children can vary the environment to satisfy their needs. When the things in an environment are organic and able to change with the child's developmental evolution, the environment has the characteristics of all living matter. Nothing in the physical world stays static. Even the rock of Gibraltar is worn away by the winds of the seas and pounded at by the force of the tides. Childhood is a progression of cognition, and the physical content of a child's environment must be open-ended enough to allow for the dynamics of that progression.

What is out there is often strong impetus for children. Very young children rarely express boredom, for at that time more than any other play comes more from the stimulation in the external world. While parents must provide a cocoon of safety, an environment must be flexible enough to stretch beyond what is pragmatic.

During the first six years of life children gain mastery of their body and its functions. In the chaotic, undifferentiated beginning of infancy, need, self, and the world are inseparable. At seven years old, a child is rational and culturally savvy. A huge amount of information and experiences are inculcated to a child between these ages. How appropriately you provide for that climb into selfness will determine the ease with which your child makes that climb.

The Five Senses

Feng shui teaches us that when all senses are engaged, a human being becomes fully occupied and generally has a higher level of contentment than when some sensory experiences are absent. A playroom must contain a variety of items that inspire a child to look, hear, smell, and touch, plus there must be room to move about. In feng shui we say that the more gravity an environment has, the more likely it is that it will be utilized and appreciated. When every sensory system is engaged forcefully, a space becomes metaphorically alive. As said before, children gravitate to an engaging space, one that is filled with sounds, moving objects, options, light, breezes, and bouquets of agreeable scents.

Simulating nature's unfolding inside is a goal. I am not suggesting dragging furniture around weekly, but am proposing circulating toys, posters, and games so that a revisit can pique a child's interest.

Sound

Movements that set air molecules into motion produce sound. Air currents vibrate against the eardrum, making the tiny bones in the inner ear trigger tiny nerve cells to send their messages to the brain. Poet/researcher/writer Diane Ackerman says in her book *A Natural History of the Senses*, "Of all the senses, hearing most resembles a contraption some ingenious plumber has put together from spare parts." She reminds us that we first know our mothers before birth by sound, just as mothers will have the very first image of their babies through the wonder of ultrasound. Hearing serves many different purposes throughout the course of a lifetime: survival, communication, entertainment, learning, and emotional expression.

In nature, our original habitat, there are always a variety of sounds. Not only do we hear a multitude of different kinds of sounds, but also we hear them intermittently. Dead silence can foster a sense of isolation in a child.

A playroom needs a heartbeat just as living things do, because children can feel the lack of life in a space and recoil from it or wither. Provide a heartbeat in a playroom by installing one or more of the following:

cuckoo clock
bubbling fish tank
wind chimes in motion
whirling fan

When I was ten years old my parents tried to send me to a private school. Previously unaware of my fate, I was startled one day when my mother unexpectedly announced that we were to visit a new school. A wave of dizziness engulfed me. It was as if a thick curtain snapped shut around me, cutting off my auditory awareness. My terror made the world eerily silent.

Arriving at the ivy-covered brick building days later, we were ushered into the principal's office. After a rather brief interview, we were escorted through the building. Our footsteps echoed as we walked along a hallway with its highly polished linoleum flooring. The principal's voice, a breathy whisper, made my own voice's deep tones seem like a ship sounding a foghorn. I heard not a single human voice emanating from the row of classrooms in the corridor. Engulfed in a morgue-like silence, I vowed never to attend that school.

Music creates an ambiance, if not exactly a heartbeat in a room. In the same way as the quality of conversation can be diminished when a television is on, constant music with lyrics can diminish imaginative thinking and communication. Although a variety of sounds from radio, tapes, and CDs can be a delightful part of playing for a period of time, you might want to utilize a timer for switching music on and off intermittently. Don't substitute music for a heartbeat.

Music

It appears that the influences of music start way before birth. As Don Campbell writes in *The Mozart Effect*, "Embryologists agree on the fact that the ear is the first organ to develop in an embryo, becomes functional after only eighteen weeks, and listens actively from twenty-four weeks on." What a child hears in utero can be learned later in life with great ease. The music a pregnant woman listens to can calm or agitate an unborn child.

Music can be used as a reward for appropriate actions. As an example, a teacher I know, Miss Miller, will play a soothing tune on the piano when her high-spirited students return from recess. If they disregard decorum she will stop playing. It is amazing how the children regulate each other's behavior in order to hear the melody uninterrupted.

Playing music is one way to attract a child to a space. When Luke was small his mother would spread out a rug in any room and surround him with books and toys. Nearby a radio with tape deck played selections of quiet, peaceful vocals. It impressed me how this combination of playthings and music kept him happily occupied for great stretches of time.

Teachers of preschoolers tell me that music is a tool of choice used to create moods. Children respond intuitively to the tempo and character of the music. Many of us can remember the marching songs played at beginning of a school's day as well as the soothing, plaintive moan of taps closing a camp's day.

Motivate, activate, and inspire your child with upbeat, joyous sounds during times when bad weather impedes outdoor time, and follow up with selections of relaxing, calming, and soothing music. Feng shui teaches us that when conditions create a deviation from the equilibrium we need to supply alternatives to balance the environment.

Scent

The nose never sleeps. The sense of smell cannot be turned off and is active all the time. Therefore, all the scents of your home transmit their messages continually. Although there is a hormone in the nose that cleanses a fragrance after a short time and prevents us from consciously smelling it, a scent continues to communicate even when its fragrance is not apparent.

In infancy we smell our caretakers before we see clearly them. The association of smell with our formative experiences plays a major role in the powerful unconscious messages smell communicates later in life. Our body reacts by the associations we have made with smells. Generations of people born in the era of plastic toys covet the scent of plastic because of its pleasant association in childhood.

Humans react to scent on a very primary level, since this sensory system is the most primitive we have. The olfactory system is literally a separate part of our brain, sitting outside the cranial bone. Scent cannot be intellectualized; it is nearly impossible to describe an actual fragrance with words unrelated to the sense they're dependent upon. Try describing the smell of lavender without using any words associated with taste or smell.

It is important to remember that from birth on a child should be surrounded with a variety of scents. Consistent use of fragrances during these formative years is the best course of action. Don't change brands of soaps, detergents, cleaning fluids, perfume or after-shave during your child's first years. The memories of a childhood home that are associated with specific scents are like a security blanket that can be carried with your child throughout life.

Every scent communicates a complex layer of information. Many books have been written about the language of scents. My personal favorite is Gabriel Mojay's book *Aromatherapy for Healing the Spirit* (published in the United Kingdom by Gaia Books, Ltd.; distributed in the United States by Inner Traditions). It is the most comprehensive, well researched book I have come across on how the scent of vegetation affects people on all levels—physical, emotional, and spiritual. In it Mojay describes the emotional and physical benefits of many scents and gives historical references to substantiate them. Here's a brief encapsulation of the material, along with other information that presents the benefits and characteristics of many common scents.

Fruits

Lemon adds zest while clarifying negative thoughts; alleviates boredom.

Tangerine invigorates while inviting a feeling of comfort; beneficial when a child has a cold.

Apple lowers blood pressure and calms; can subdue tantrums or frustration.

Grapefruit can alleviate resentment; beneficial during cleanup.

Spices

Marjoram eases feelings of emotional isolation that cause insomnia and grief. Marjoram is beneficial when parents are going out for the evening.

Ginger can help manifest drive and the will to achieve for those with unactualized plans; beneficial during cleanup or when a child feels bored.

Rosemary is a confidence builder because it empowers the mind; beneficial anytime.

Coriander can ease potential despondency when a child does not have many options for play because of illness or other circumstances.

Fennel unlocks the ability to express things without inhibition; can help a shy child express himself or herself with others.

Flowers

Geranium stabilizes a child who is in a frenzy or is engaged in activities agitatedly.

Jasmine lifts confidence; beneficial for socializing with new groups.

Lavender reduces shyness and the likelihood of sudden outbursts of anger, reaches all emotional ranges and feelings, and is a general tonic.

Trees and Bushes

Eucalyptus dispels feeling cooped up.

Pine restores feeling positive about oneself.

Laurel aids concentration and memory; beneficial when activities require memorizing.

Cypress helps alleviate boredom.

Touch

Consider how very sensitive the surface of a child's skin is compared with adults'. Adults may be able to prick the bottoms of their feet and not feel a thing. But children's skin has not been toughened by exposure to the elements, so their entire skin surface is more sensitive. Every contact with another surface engages us in subconscious ways, and in feng shui we can explain it. Therefore, be aware of the kinds of materials you bring into a playroom and where you place them. Variety is desirable, but make sure that the message a texture exudes complements the activity it accompanies.

Rough Surfaces

A surface scratchy to the touch is in feng shui related to the fire element. Many upholstery fabrics for sofas and chairs have a stain-resistant fiber that is not only rough but almost greasy to the touch. If calming and relaxing is the desired effect, do not furnish a playroom with such fibers.

Cool and Soft Surfaces

We rarely give children slippery fabrics to play with. A fabric like silk is hard to grasp and hold onto. However, in warm weather, consider furnishing a playroom with this type of fabric for its cooling effect on a child who cuddles in it. Moreover, slick materials can act as a motivation for movement. When covered with a slippery fabric, the slightest incline can become a slide.

Hard Surfaces

Surfaces that resist being manipulated or that cannot be moved when sat upon and touched feel supportive. In practicing the principles of feng shui, we use firm surfaces where a person needs to feel guarded and safe. The human preference for sleeping on a firm surface is understandable in terms of the need for feeling secure during the vulnerable period of sleep. A surface that is compact to the touch resonates with the earth element and can add a feeling of security to a playroom. Thus, a very large ball, a cube wrapped in cloth, or any large object that supports physical resistance is good to have in a play area.

Soft and Cushy Fabrics

Materials that envelop are naturally associated with childhood. Children love to romp around wrapped in blankets, hurtle themselves upon mounds of pillows, and fling themselves headlong across a room into a receptive sofa or chair. The availability of soft, cushy materials for them to shape adds a wonderful dimension to a play area. Stack pillows in a corner, scatter them around, or toss them on a seating unit. Your children will discover many ways to integrate them into their play.

Sight

What we see provides us with approximately 70 percent of the information about our surroundings.

Color

The choice of colors is an important way to tweak an environment to ensure that its visual messages are appropriate. I suggest you begin to think of ways to rotate colors to alter your child's playroom as needs arise. Use items that are easily moved to provide a surface for the colors you choose. Here's a list of furnishings you can use for quick color changes:

cloths over chests   tablecloths draped on stools
area rugs   afghans
small chairs   pillows
umbrellas

While the purpose of most of the items on this list is self-evident, that of umbrellas and tablecloths may not be. An umbrella is useful for creating a room within a room. Placed in a stand or hanging from the ceiling, it can shape a small, cozy area for quiet play. In a home with many children, it can be a private retreat when a child wants to be left alone. It can also serve as a home base for a game of tag. In addition, hung from the ceiling an umbrella creates a cavelike niche that caters to activities such as reading or napping.

Use items from the list above to furnish a playroom. Following is a discussion of how to choose colors for those items for the most appropriate elemental effect.

Use an umbrella to create a niche for reading or napping.

Fire spurs a child to action. **Fire's red and orange** are colors that support large motor activities, prompt physical energy, and generally infuse a playroom with dynamic forces. These are absolutely the wrong colors to use when you want a child to be relaxed, quiet, and focused. Use fire's red or orange to

stimulate physical action when a child is playing alone
cheer and warm a large or cool space
encourage mental animation for make-believe

Colors of safety, **earth's brown, mustard, and tan** evoke a feeling of protection when used on walls or the furnishings placed against the walls. Should a child need this kind of security or stability, these are good colors to use for the room's overall effect. A reading area will benefit from a feeling of comfort with a rug, pillow, or throw containing these colors. Use earth's brown, mustard, and tan

when a child plays alone
in areas requiring mental concentration
to promote calm

Shiny colors mesmerize children. If an area is underused or if you want to steer a child to a specific area, **metal's silver, gold, copper, and shiny white** will attract the child, spurring him or her to check such an area out. When a child needs help with focus, the metallic colors will bolster his or her ability to make choices. Use metal's silver, gold, copper, and shiny white

around areas used for small motor activities, such as puzzles
in areas where a child has a hard time sustaining activity
in rooms without a great deal of natural light

The effect of **water's blue and black** on an environment ranges from freedom to instability. Light blue creates a feeling of spaciousness, while black can make a space disappear. A black area carpet or flooring can actually make a floor appear hole-like and therefore unstable. Confronted by these two color messages, a child may feel anything from free to unstable. Faber Birren has shown that the color blue actually lowers blood pressure and heartbeat in adults. Blue creates an atmosphere that supports centering. An overly exuberant child can benefit from the calming effect of the blue palette, while a child with a physical motor disability will feel even less stable with black. Keep in mind the variation of blue and black messages:

- Light blue creates a feeling of spaciousness.
- Medium blue helps a child engage in solo activities.
- Medium to dark blue establishes focus in a messy area of a room.
- Dark blue tempers enthusiasm.
- Black reduces stability and exudes emptiness.

Use water's blue or black in these ways: Use a round black carpet as a boundary to prevent children from going to an unsafe area. Use blue in a napping area to reduce excitement.

Nothing promotes more mental and physical activity than **wood's green**. Don't be surprised by the natural exuberance green infuses into a décor. Its role in a playroom is therefore very important. However, rather than using green for flat surfaces such as walls, furniture, or flooring, I recommend you use it with moving objects. In this way green will supply the message of nature, where green is a dominant color and where stillness is minimum. Use wood's green

in mobiles
with plants
as lightweight curtains, so long as a breeze is permitted to enter

Mirrors

Children and animals are fascinated by seeing their reflections. Children mug and prance in front of mirrors, especially when installed at their height. Children rarely have a source of reflection they can both see themselves in from the ground up and approach nose to nose.

Position a mirror in a playroom directly at floor level. It will provide a great deal of pleasure, especially with a chest of dress-up clothes nearby. I have a picture etched in my memory and also have a photograph of my son all decked out in a muffler worn as a hat, rows of colorful beads, white gloves, and lipstick. From the age of three children delight in pretense. A mirror can be their best accessory.

Install a mirror at floor level in your child's playroom.

I once owned a house where I mounted a mirror on the back of the kitchen's lower cabinets that faced a dining room area. My thinking was that the mirror would lighten the weighty feeling imposed by this contiguous surface of the cabinets. I was pleased with the results, but over the years I learned volumes about other benefits of installing mirrors at the height of young children and pets.

Playrooms and the Three Stages of Childhood

You may want to plan your child's playroom to accommodate his or her age. Children have different needs from playrooms depending on which of the three stages of childhood they are in.

The Me, Myself, and I Stage (Birth to Eighteen Months)

During infancy children are defenseless and at the mercy of their immediate environment. A crawling infant may discover how to slide backward to descend a staircase instead of tumbling down it, but that same child might not know not to shake a table supporting a bowl of hot soup. Your first consideration in planning a playroom must be safety. Be sure your infant's playroom includes these conditions:

- no chemicals or household cleaning products in lower cabinets, drawers, or shelves
- no easily accessible electrical wires that when pulled could tumble a heavy object
- no knives, metal pokers, or objects that can be jabbed into electrical sockets
- no cement or stone floors left uncovered
- double-hung windows that can be locked securely in place when open
- no continuous artificial noise such as television or stereo
- not decorated entirely with bright, bold colors

At the Me, Myself, and I stage imitation is a form of learning. Parents will be amazed when observing their child's inborn ability to mirror the actions, tones, and expressions of those who interact with them.

This fact was brought home to me when I was visiting an eighteen-month-old friend. We sat on the sofa and played a silly game of me lunging toward him as if intending to tickle him and him jumping away screaming with laughter and delight. The child wanted to repeat the game over and over. We continued playing this game on and off during my hour-long visit. Even afterward, whenever he saw me he would immediately replay his role of giggling and jumping away in the hope I would respond in my role by pretending to go after him to tickle him.

Thus, an enjoyable pattern is easy to instill in a child at this stage. The aptitude for imitation of a child at this stage is connected with the forces of organic development; enjoyable repetitive play creates a positive link to the nerves and the sensory system.

It's tough to separate children from their caretakers unless they're sufficiently engaged and stimulated by other activities. The easiest way to do this, by far, is having them watch television or videos. There is a time and place for television. There certainly is programming for children that entertains and supports positive self-esteem and values. The trick is to use it as an electronic babysitter only *occasionally*.

Try to engage in activities with your children. Or allow your children to join you in your activities. At this stage, the value of engaging in real activities far outweighs some play ones. A play or toy kitchen will most likely go unused while spoons and pots and pans in the real kitchen will be enthusiastically enjoyed.

The value of a playroom at this stage of development is diminished unless you are willing to spend time there. The good news is that before you run to decorate a special room for play, you have one and a half years to discern your child's special needs in order to shape a play space that suits him or her.

The Magician Stage (Eighteen Months to Three Years)

At eighteen months, a child has gained some mastery over mobility and dexterity. This is when self-involved activities begin. Although early during this stage your child may display some of that tagalong, "I want to do what you are doing" behavior, now is the time to provide a playroom to accommodate self-involved activities.

Making a Mess

Having an area that supports filling and emptying is imperative for children during this stage. Be it sand in a bucket, rocks in a bowl, toys in a chest, or water in a cup, nothing is as fascinating as dragging something out and putting it back. An area for messy activities or a contained space where cleanup is reasonably easy is a benefit. Flooring in this area must be sturdy and able to withstand scarring, water, grit, and dirt.

An enterprising couple I know built a plywood play box and placed it in the corner of their children's playroom. They glued inexpensive linoleum inside this shallow box and covered the walls adjacent to the messy box with colorful plastic tablecloths. The two-year-old twins had a field day with all kinds of activities and materials not happily integrated in other areas of a home. Their mom was free from fear of having irreversible damage done to her home. When the twins were about five the box became unnecessary, and I remember the Jackson Pollock–like look of the flooring just before it was removed.

Whether you build a box or just use temporary coverings, nothing is more delightful to a child than a space in which to play in a messy way without restraint. A playroom should have a messy area.

Building and Shaping

Exploring feats of balance and forming shapes begins during this stage. The bigger the shapes, the better. To accommodate this activity, purchase inexpensive blocks or second-hand sofa cushions. The types of block building materials that have an impact on the whole body are very seductive. Pillows, sheets, and large foam blocks, which can be built up, tumbled over, and cuddled up to, can serve mental and large motor activities nicely.

Free Space

A space left completely empty is a benefit. In order to let your children learn to shape their lives, allow them to shape a space to suit their needs and spark their imagination. Having unencumbered space to jump, run, or tumble around in offers into the mix of indoor activities the chance to use large motor skills. Some children absolutely require this kind of movement. Open spaces are places to shape materials into all sorts of large-scale projects. A group of children can while away countless hours building a special universe, using every available toy and block if there is available space.

The On the Road to Reason Stage (Three to Six Years)

A child is ready for more complexity during the On the Road to Reason stage of development. Simply providing materials like sand, clay, and pliable wires is not enough. Now a child is capable of experiencing how these materials change with variations of temperature, liquid, and pigment. A dish with ice cubes or a box with a light inside can be a forum for experiment.

Transformability and flexibility are ingredients that shouldn't be excluded in planning a play space. Having a rigid, nontransmutable space that cannot be shaped according to a child's mood and development may be reinforcing a pattern of rigidity in the face of options. Include the following items in a playroom to increase the space's transformability:

screens
furniture that stores
furniture on wheels
chairs that revolve
small area carpets

A playroom for children at this stage needs lightweight, culture-neutral, nonspecific items that can be transformed into creations of a child's vision. "The more flash and bang a toy comes with, the less opportunity that toy has to be used as something else," says Marcie Gitman, early childhood environmental education coordinator for the Minnesota Children's

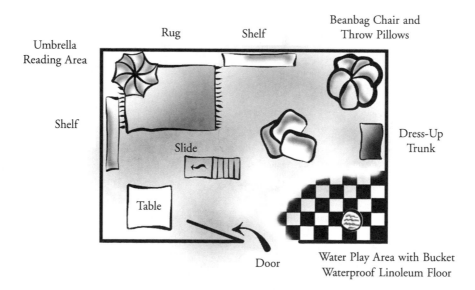

Furnish a child's playroom with items that allow for flexibility.

Many years ago I was privileged to view an installation of a hundred or so cloth-covered foam cubes at a children's museum. The various-size cubes were stacked haphazardly in a huge pile. Then the children were let loose. They squealed in delight at being able to throw themselves into this massive structure with abandon. Also, the children were encouraged to alter the shape to suit their whim. In no time at all, children altered the structure into many different landscapes for play: igloo-type cocoons, bridges on which to roll or walk, forts, roadways, and rockets. It seemed as if every conceivable fantasy was capable of being realized with these blocks of foam.

Museum. "It's important for children to have a balance between toys with a specific purpose and those objects that can be turned into anything." Parents can foster their children's creativity by providing basic, everyday items kids can use to create their own adventures.

The old story about a child playing with the box the present came in instead of the present itself has real truth to it. The cardboard box your new stove came in can be a spaceship, a house, a cave, or anything a child can dream up. But a fire truck will be only a fire truck; most children will not see it as a school bus or a dump truck. Kids need some things to be open-ended to use as tools along their path of creative learning.

Here's a list of materials to keep handy to squelch boredom in kids who complain about having "nothing to do":

paper, both plain white and colored construction paper	pipe cleaners
finger paints	cotton balls
markers or crayons	clothespins
blocks	old clothes (even old towels or pillowcases will do)
scraps of cloth, felt, and foam	paper bags
ribbon and yarn	cardboard boxes

You may remember that as an older child, admitting to being bored gave your parents the opportunity to give you something to do. That "something to do" was not a trip to a zoo or new toy or game. "Something to do" meant scrubbing the kitchen floor, mowing the lawn, or washing the family car. So, unlike many kids today, you may have learned to take charge of your boredom. There is nothing wrong with letting children be bored. Boredom leads to exploration, which in turn leads to creativity.

To play is to invent life. After all, isn't that what we all long to have—a life that feels like play?

14

Bedrooms

No other room is more exclusively designated for a child than the bedroom. A bedroom is more than a sleeping compartment. It should include not only age-appropriate items but also those unique conditions that express a child's individual nature. It should house things that tantalize, contain things to explore, and be a secure, safe place.

Logistics

Traditionally, family bedrooms were located in one contiguous area in a home. They were either upstairs or on one side of a home's main gathering area. But in homes today there is more variation. Distinctions between different bedrooms include size, views, and proximity to the parents' bedroom and hall bathroom. The significance assigned to the differences may be important.

View

When I was a child, the views from my and my sister's bedrooms were dramatically different. Mine was the one facing the backyard. Underneath my bedroom window was a sloping roof that met a descending hill. With little effort I could slide from the roof to the ground without fear of hurting myself. By the age of seven I found this exit irresistible and escaped many times unbeknownst to my parents. Moreover, the view beyond the backyard was a wooded scene uninterrupted by any human-made structures. My childhood's scene was awash with nature.

My sister, on the other hand, faced the front of our home. Ever the sentinel, she recorded the comings and goings of visitors, could recite timetables of neighbors' routines, and knew all the dogs whose owners walked them past the house.

Both of us have etched in our memory of place those scenes viewed from our bedroom windows. I am certain that their influence has been long-lasting and potent, for my sister grew up to watch over theatrical events as a producer and I have lived the bulk of my adult life on a dirt road in a country home whose panorama is not troubled by buildings, roads, or electric poles. I think each of us had the scene that balanced our very different personalities. I was the outgoing child and needed a contemplative view. My sister, who was reserved, was bolstered by the more socially vibrant scene outside her window.

Consider the scenes outside your child's bedroom window and what they may transmit. The following table of my impressions is a forum for your reflection.

Bedroom Window Views

VIEW	POSITIVE EFFECT	CHALLENGING EFFECT
Street scene	Sociability	Distrust of people or desire to escape
Flowering tree	Belief in renewal	Sadness at fleeting beauty
Uninterrupted lawn	Life's blank canvas	Boredom
Woods	Love of diversity	Lack of control
Side of a building	Protection by others	Closed in by others
Interior courtyard	Secure and safe	Self-centeredness
Mountains	Inspiration of discovery	Limits exploration
Ocean	Zest and excitment	An impenetrable barrier
River	Belief in change	Fear of abandonment
Gardens with variety	Diversity as a benefit	Overwhelming possibilities

Size

After view, size is a factor. Bigger is not always better, although in feng shui we are aware that bigger is experienced as more powerful. However, features of a smaller room can offset its lack of space and make it desirable. Look at a child's room as a cube, not just a flat square. Create opportunities for children to move vertically as well as horizontally. If the cubic footage is fully utilized, then even the smallest bedroom becomes a big enough arena for the many activities children engage in. Mount sturdy, open-weave netting on a wall to create a climbing wall, if only to a height of three feet. Moving laterally on the netting is as much fun for a child as moving vertically. Use soft pillows or mats as flooring to soften any falls. Or, hang a thick, knotted rope over your child's bed from one of the ceiling's supportive beams for an indoor swing. Step ladders can serve play as well as accessibility to elevated surfaces such as sleeping lofts and bunk beds, two more ideas for getting the most from a small bedroom.

Sleeping Lofts

Lofts don't have to be more than chest high. If you are handy, create a sleeping platform in your child's bedroom with four-by-four uprights. If not, catalogs from retailers like Ikea have inexpensive modular furniture. The space created underneath is the kind of small, cozy place children love. Children generally like sleeping in a loft. My son spent his whole early childhood in a loft over our kitchen that opened onto our main gathering area. One advantage was that he never whined about going to bed. Another was that he has never been a light sleeper because overhearing conversation was standard in his bedroom.

Bunk Beds

The simplest alternative to a loft is bunk beds. Either one of the bunks can be a secret space for an individual child or a play space for a small group. There is something mysteriously delicious about having a completely enclosable space. Hang a blanket from the upper bunk or mount or tape a curtain on the ceiling above to turn a bunk bed into Ali Baba's cave.

Setting Up a New Bedroom

Just before Sean was two, he moved to new home. His parents had no intention of purchasing new furniture, bed linens, or artwork for his room. The only difference between his former bedroom and the new was its location. In the old house his bedroom was next to his parents', and in the new one it was on the opposite side of the house. To lessen the potential confusion and sense of isolation, I suggested that his bed and wall hangings be set up in the same position in relation to the door as they had been formerly. This way he would have only one new component to deal with, that of negotiating the route to his parents' bedroom.

The key to a smooth transition is in retaining something familiar. Too many alterations can be unsettling. If you want to refurbish your child's bedroom, do so after an adjustment period, not right after the move. The most important constant is the relationship of the head of the bed to the entrance door.

Furnishings

Generally, a bedroom should have the following items:

something to sleep on
place to store clothes
place to store toys
shelves to house books, toys,
    and dolls
seating for an adult
flat surface for tabletop
    activities

manageable window treatment
easy-to-clean flooring with soft,
    comfortable, washable area rugs
overall lighting supplemented by
    wall-mounted or tabletop accent
    lamps
empty chest or shelf to accommodate new interests

The last item is important, for feng shui teachings enlighten us with the knowledge that empty spaces are necessary to support expanding interests and embrace change. Rotate items or give away what children have outgrown to encourage them to stretch themselves toward new interests.

Positioning of the Bed

In all cases a bed must be positioned with the child's head facing the entrance door. If any more than a slight turn of his or her head is required to see the entrance of the bedroom when he or she is in bed, relocate the bed. You can free up a great deal of floor space by placing a bed with two of its sides against the walls farthest from the door.

Cribs

A crib is an infant's cocoon. What is placed in the crib and around the room is food for the developing mind. A child arrives in the world with a

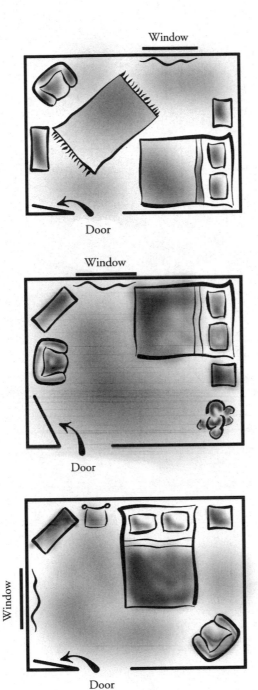

Position the bed opposite the bedroom's entrance. More floor space is free when two sides of a bed are against the wall farthest from the entrance door.

propensity for being active, passive, cranky, or docile. Outfit the physical atmosphere to balance these general characteristics. For example, a colicky baby would be well served with large fields of yin colors to soothe, and a docile child would be supported by a pattern of many small repeats to reflect upon.

Hang pictures, textiles, and other objects that sharply contrast with the wall's color on the walls surrounding the crib. As previously stated, infants have an easier time distinguishing objects if there is contrast. A variety of colors, shapes, sounds, and textures stimulate an infant's appetite to investigate.

The sides of a crib can provide stimulation also. An inventive client of mine mounted curtain tracks on the ceiling above her daughter's crib. From the track she hung painted Ping-Pong balls, lightweight mobiles, feathers, and bells. A small fan on the floor animated this cheerful collection. The need to wind up or replace the batteries of a kinetic mobile was eliminated. These dancing forms fascinated this baby. She was entertained during the day and lulled to sleep each night by their colorful and kinetic presence. When she learned to sit and stand up my client changed the suspended toys to those that the child could manipulate and put in her mouth, such as wheels, rubber toys with movable parts, sound-making playthings, and Nerf balls. Another happy consequence was that the child delightedly whacked her playthings around for long periods, never seeming to tire of this game.

Here are some more suggestions for furnishings around and inside cribs:

Use blankets with a variety of textures.
Hang or mount nonelectric sound machines on crib slats.
Place movable toys, such as mobiles, wheels, or loosely jointed
    stuffed animals nearby.
Wrap several crib slats with plush fabric.
Hang lightweight items over or alongside the crib to provide stimu-
    lation.
Install a CD player nearby to play music.

Flooring

Practicality and comfort are key ingredients for a floor in a child's bedroom. I might as well state my prejudice against wall-to-wall carpeting in children's bedrooms right now: if flooring does not afford the opportunity for both wet and dry play, then it is limiting. While I don't expect a floor to be hosed down, I do expect children to feel free to experiment with paints, clay, plants, and other items that may require the use of water in the privacy of their own rooms. While other areas in a home, namely the kitchen, bathroom, or outdoors, serve water-related activities better, a bedroom's flooring should be flexible enough to occasionally serve such purposes. If bedrooms are to serve as havens for children, they must allow for a full range of activities. Perhaps some children don't use their bedrooms because they have to give up the activities that are permitted elsewhere at home. You may remember wanting to stay outside longer than your parents thought was advisable. Was part of your reluctance due to the fact that being inside was more limiting than being outdoors? In the same way, if a bedroom serves fewer purposes than other rooms, it will be less desirous—flooring is often a room's most limiting factor.

A bedroom floor should

have a smooth surface for sliding, building with blocks, or drawing
provide a comfortable place for quiet activities such as reading or
    resting
have pillows or mats for safety during jumping, rolling, and other
    physical activities
be easy to clean thoroughly to eliminate mold, bacteria, and dust
have some space for messy play such as painting, water activities,
    and plant or animal care

One kind of flooring that meets the above criteria is linoleum covered with one or several washable area rugs made from cotton. You want to pile two or three rugs together, creating a squashy, comfortable surface.

Window Treatments

While windows pierce the opaqueness of walls, allowing us to look out, they also puncture the security of the contiguous wall. Should a window be located behind the head of a bed, provide a very secure window treatment, such as shutters with a latch. If a window is on the side of the bed, a more versatile window treatment is sufficient. Bedroom window treatments should both screen a view and be translucent. This would necessitate a two-tier treatment, such as a light-obscuring curtain over a venetian blind.

Window treatments that can be easily manipulated by a young child are preferable. Blinds that require pulling up while pushing off to one side cause a young child frustration. Curtains on large rings over smooth poles can be easily pulled aside and give a child the mastery essential for confidence.

Window Seats

Probably the most underutilized and intriguing window feature is a window seat. So long as a window can be securely locked and there is no possibility a child could open it, then this is an enchanting feature. A couple of pillows, a blanket, and a good toy or book on a window seat can turn a dreary day into an enchanted one. Children gain more intimate visual contact with the scene outside the window from the proximity a window seat affords. A view from a window seat offers new dimensions to detail, like observing nature through binoculars.

A bedroom is like a piece of jewelry, a small exquisite personal expression set against a context of the background. It is a child's first experience of selfhood in a physical form. Children may own the same toys or clothes or go to the same school as others, but each bedroom has the opportunity to be uniquely personal. It is up to you to uncover your child's inner voice.

15

The Great Outdoors

What wonders await the eyes, heart, and mind of those who explore the earth? There could not be a more fertile source for a child's imagination than outside in nature. All the ingredients that feng shui seeks to replicate inside are readily available outside.

The component that makes nature so compelling is proportion. Children do not ponder the oversized scenes with as much rapture as they do the intimate, manageable, detailed, and small. To a child the grand scenes seem out of focus, hardly discernable, and merely abstractions that don't permit as much integration, enmeshment, and involvement. You can hide in a group of bushes, smell their aroma, and investigate a leaf's veins, but a distant ridge is only a picture that doesn't deliver anything tangible.

> To create a manageable space for children to explore, throw a rope in a circle or place a hula hoop on the earth to create a boundary for investigation. Suggest they collect different stones, flowers, or blades of grass. Setting limits can help children focus on the small and not be overstimulated by the expanse of outdoors.

The Natural Environment

Naturalists Gary Nabhan and Stephen Trimble write in their book *The Geography of Childhood* that one-quarter of the children born in the United States in this next generation will start their lives in urban slums and never experience the land upon which food is grown. So many children will never have a firsthand experience with flowers, shrubs, trees, grasses, birds, or other animals living wild in nature. Certainly your children can't experience everything under the sun, but it is vital that you expose them to as much experience of nature as possible.

Nature affords unabashed freedom for the child. A child can't ruin much outdoors that will call forth an adult's wrath. Sure, she can step on a flowerbed, make a bike tire rut in a wet lawn, or ignore a sign not to pick the flowers, but nature provides a random abundance that precludes, in most cases, destruction by children.

There are many activities that do not harm the natural terrain. Toss a pebble into the water, and surely the pebble will not be missed. Children can climb trees to examine a hollow, roll down an incline, and carry buckets of water from a stream to a hole dug in the earth; no harm will befall the environment. These are all activities that are either forbidden or need close supervision indoors, but outside they are far less restricted.

The freedom afforded by the diversity and indestructibility of the outdoors is a gift to all children. No climatic conditions should preclude children's being outside. When properly dressed children can explore year-round. If you don't live near undeveloped lands, plan trips to wild places—forests,

> *I spent my first seven years in Brooklyn, where cement replaced dirt and lawns were wild lands. I remember my astonishment the first time I saw a tomato growing on a vine. I could hardly believe that a slim green stick could support the weight of the plump, red fruit. I was further mystified the first time I was taken to the coast of New England. My dad pointed at a large fish and told me that what I saw was a tuna. With disbelief I scoffed, "Dad, it's too big for the can." I had not had enough real experiences in nature.*

seasides, meadows, green areas, and parks—that don't bear as much human intervention as others. Playgrounds are fine and fun because they provide a place for much-needed large motor skill activities, but they cannot replace nature's playground.

The unique feature about nature is the element of surprise. Seeing a frog huddling under a rock, a lizard scampering out from the underbrush, and a bit of fool's gold glimmering from a rock is the kind of adventure that children cherish. We tend to keep things in the same place indoors, and although there is comfort in predictability, it can become monotonous.

Animals

Critters, so abundant outdoors, are fascinating to children. Children find ants marching in lines, grasshoppers jumping, and squirrels dashing about endlessly engaging. Sometimes a child's enthusiasm for having a pet abates as soon as the pet is brought home. I rarely saw Alison play with her rabbit in the house. Yet Alison's interest in her pet ignited when she brought it outside. She and the rabbit could play for hours. She would uncage the rabbit and follow it as it merrily hopped around the yard. Apparently the rabbit's affection for Alison was strong enough to prevent it from straying. Rabbit and child were deeply engaged in playing together in the wilds of the suburbs.

Since wild critters cannot all be pets, you can create habitats that would be visible from a child's indoor play space. Regula, my literary agent, has fourteen bird feeders and three suet dispensers on her property. All windows frame the wildlife that flocks to these feeding stations. I once consulted for a New England family with an asthmatic child who loved animals but was highly allergic to them. My feng shui remedy was for them to hang bird feeders, plant flowers that attracted butterflies, and set up squirrel food dispensers and deer licks outside her bedroom windows.

Trees

Think about the benefits of a tree. They are climbed upon, hidden behind, and used as shelter, landmarks, and privacy barriers. A tree's leaves provide a dazzling array of shadows on the ground and a kaleidoscope of shapes against the sky. Tree leaves are fascinating to handle. A child can examine their intricate veins, feel their textures, and smell their scent. Fall leaves can be piled, tossed, kicked, crumbled, and used for collages. What object indoors provides such diverse opportunities? Even a felled tree provides materials for fort building and a place for acrobatic ventures, dens of little animals, or colonies of mushrooms. If you are lucky enough to have a yard surrounding your home, plant a tree. Choose a fast-growing variety or perhaps a fruit tree whose limbs remain close to the ground. No bought object can beat the medley of opportunities of these stately live umbrellas.

Natural habitats are the grounds upon which a child can be the architect. Children's interaction with nature is a partnership, just like that of painter and canvas, musician and instrument, welder and metal. Indoors the environment is formed and conceived by adults to meet social, economic, and cultural needs. Outdoors children have every opportunity to explore the depth of their personage, the height of daring—and the satisfaction of knowing that they are not creating a mess. Outdoors the canvas is blank and intervention is as large as the imagination of the inventor. The natural world is a place for personal freedom.

16

Special Needs

This chapter's discussion is confined to children's special needs resulting from physical limitations. In the spirit of creating a barrier-free environment, it is necessary to be aware of what obstacles may impede movement for a child who has special needs. Even if none of your children have unique needs, they may befriend someone who does.

What is a barrier? A barrier is any space that is too small to move through, too hard to manipulate, or too high or too low to reach.

To appreciate the barriers faced by a child with a disability, try this exercise. Imagine not having the use of your legs and hands while you try to negotiate an icy pathway bordered by an overgrown thorny hedge to the stairs leading to a home's door. Consider what would be required for you to safely reach the destination. How would you avoid the prickly vegetation? How would you ascend the stairs? Lift a door knocker or push the doorbell? Knowledge of what may be considered a barrier helps as you begin the process of shaping a space in which a child with physical disabilities can thrive.

Consider the following questions when shaping a space that can feel friendly to anyone, especially children.

Is the route of travel stable, firm, and slip-resistant?

Are area carpets taped down? Any flooring that can be lifted is a potential hazard. Are there treads on the threshold of rooms that can be tripped over? Treads designed to transition one type of flooring with another often have a raised lip on both sides. If a child has difficulty lifting his or her feet, it can literally be a stumbling block.

Even if the flooring is not slippery, it feels unstable if it has a high sheen. In fact, I normally recommend that hospital lobbies do not have highly polished floors, as they magnify feelings of insecurity.

Are routes throughout a home wide enough?

Thirty-six inches is a good rule of thumb as a minimum clearance for a single wheelchair to maneuver safely. But the minimum width should be considerably greater to enable two children to scamper about side by side.

Are the objects that protrude into a route safe and easy to see?

Pointed corners on furniture, plants, vines, branches, sculptures, or other objects, easy for a child with normal agility and sight to sidestep, can be a challenge to a child with special needs.

Outdoors, a child in a wheelchair often has more room to maneuver and therefore is more at ease in regulating his or her movement to avoid an object that is in the way. But in confined spaces, be alert to those potential hazards or annoyances.

Is the passage to enter all rooms wider than thirty-two inches?

Sometimes space between the frame of a door is wide enough for a child in a wheelchair, but the door doesn't swing clear, making the space actually narrower. The culprit is usually the hinges. Install swing-clear hinges to remedy such a situation.

Are door and cabinet handles accessible from a seated position? Can they be operated with a closed fist?

Naturally this precludes knobs that must be turned. Latches that require the weight of the arm to unlatch are barrier free for any child with sufficient strength or with limited use of his or her hands.

Are there enough five-foot circles in which to turn a wheelchair completely around?

Bathrooms and kitchens are rooms where retrofitting for this need is difficult. Most other rooms have sufficient space to clear a five-foot circle to accommodate this maneuver.

Is artwork hung low enough to be visible without undue strain?

Nothing is more frustrating than being unable to see an object clearly enough to be able to enjoy it. A painting hung too high filled with small, indistinct details may trigger subconscious frustration because it is difficult to see. Over time, when a person is unable to view something, it either becomes invisible or causes resentment.

Are sufficient tabletops or counters within reach?

Providing adequately low work surfaces for toys and household items is essential. Again, bathrooms and kitchens are the spaces where retrofitting is more difficult. Clipping an extension onto an existing surface is one way to circumvent having to rebuild it. Amend existing tables and counters with hooks and hinges.

For wheelchairs, affixing a tray to a split rubber tube that can curl around the wheelchair's arms is an inexpensive and reasonably easy way to make a flexible surface for play.

Split tubes with a board attached snap onto the arms of the wheelchair.

Is there knee accessibility under work or table surfaces of at least twenty-seven inches high by thirty inches wide by nineteen inches deep?

Be conscious of the height of tables used to eat, work, and play games on. Pedestal tables are ideal, for they have fewer encumbrances to deal with. While a round table has many other advantages for families, its lack of defined edges can be annoying for a child who has limited upper body mobility.

A child who is less mobile than others requires even more sensory stimulation. For example, the home of a child with impaired vision should contain a great variety of textures, while the home of a child with impaired hearing should contain many patterns and movable accessories. Whenever there is a lack or limitation in one sensory area, emphasize others. Consider adding smells, sights, and sounds to stimulate a child with special needs.

- Add **aromas** in more places. Plug in diffusers at the threshold of each room.
- Increase the variety of **lighting**. Light pathways more intensely, and make sure that the pools of light thrown from shades are large enough to encompass the entire child.
- Add more **sounds** to the atmosphere. Mount door harps or loop bells over doorknobs, windows, or anything that moves occasionally.
- Have as much **movement** as possible. Hang mobiles under air vents or close to a door. Use lightweight curtains that billow. Attach pinwheels to a fan. Provide toys that move, like Slinky.

Some ideas for additional arm and hand manipulation are

- trapeze circles mounted to hang from beams or the ceiling
- beanbags mounted at chest height to shove, knead, and punch
- a clothesline hung to connect spaces and to use as a message sender
- a low basketball hoop

All children have "special needs," for everyone has both strengths and weaknesses. If a child can't sit still, a corner of pillows might lure her to restfulness. A plank placed between two low rungs of a ladder can be the first step in conquering a fear of heights. The way to prepare a space to fully realize a child's potential is to be honest in evaluating his or her special needs.

17

Nontoxic Homes

Children spend a great deal more time indoors today than they did in previous generations. Therefore, we must pay strict attention to the potentially hazardous toxins used to construct our homes and contained in the consumer goods we bring into our homes.

The world production of inorganic chemicals alone has grown incredibly: from 1 million tons in 1930, to 500 million in 1994, to an estimated nearly 1 billion today. These facts about materials in today's buildings may astound you. Until 1950, buildings were constructed of 60 to 70 percent neutral materials such as stone and clay and 30 to 40 percent organic materials such as wood and cork. By contrast in 1990 buildings were only 10 to 30 percent neutral, 5 percent organic, and 65 to 85 percent hard and synthetic materials such as concrete, steel, glass, and plastic.

In terms of known safety hazards, consider these facts about today's homes:

One in five has a gas leak.
One in four has a venting problem with the heating system.
One in three has undetected fungus growth.

Lack of Air Exchange

A home is like a third skin. The first is our skin, and the second is the clothes we wear. You may recall the character who was asphyxiated in the 1964 James Bond movie *Goldfinger* because the paint all over her body prevented her skin from breathing. The skin's surface releases the body's toxins, and a home must perform the same function.

In the past windows were rarely draft free and vapor barriers not so airtight. That means that a home's air was exchanged more frequently. Today a typical home might be energy efficient, but that keeps toxins from escaping along with the heat. We are strangling ourselves in our own toxins. Children are more at risk than most adults.

Symptoms

The following symptoms may be caused by an unhealthy home:

> persistent flu-like symptoms
> warm or burning face
> eye irritations
> itching, tingling, or prickling in the face or on the body
> upper respiratory dryness
> lack of concentration
> swollen mucous membranes with no virus infection

Many believe that chemicals released into the atmosphere and mold account for the rise of asthma, bronchial conditions, and other lung related conditions. Recently, I read an account of the possible triggers for autism. Toxic homes that cause the immune system to be compromised is on the list. According to Helmut Ziehe,* the answers to many medical maladies lie in the increasing use of building materials laden with toxins coupled with fibers used for clothing that are embedded with dyes, fire retardant, and other chemicals. The daily contact of a child's skin with chemically "improved" synthetics and his or her consumption of foods mixed with dyes, taste enhancers such as monosodium glutamate (MSG), stabilizers, preservatives, and other chemical additives create a perilous combination capable of causing serious health problems.

---

*Helmut Ziehe, founder of the International Institute for Bau-Biologie & Ecology, in Clearwater, Florida, has provided the facts in this chapter. If your child exhibits any of the symptoms discussed that cannot be eliminated by standard medical procedures, I suggest you call this organization at 727-461-4371 or E-mail them at baubiologie@earthlink.com.

Chemicals in Home Construction

What to do? As parents we must create an environment that houses as few toxins or potential hazards as possible. Here are a few considerations for you to reflect on, depending on your child's health and the age of your home. Homes built before 1976 contained substantially fewer hazardous materials, with the exception of lead paints. Even taking into consideration that asbestos and lead paints created grave health conditions in older homes, the fact remains that today's homes carry more toxins.

Here is just a brief list of the types of toxins and hazards we live with in our homes:

Polluting gases and vapors: Formaldehyde, carbondioxine, carbon monoxide, nitrogen oxide, sulfoxide, lead, radon, styrene, arsine, hydrogen fluoride, hydrochloric acid, polychlorinated biphenyls (PCB), polyvinylchloride, chlornaphtaline, and hundreds of other chemical substances present in polluted indoor air

Fibers: Asbestos, synthetics, microglass and microrock, and textiles

Microbes: Bacteria, fungi, and viruses

Radiation: Radioactive materials, electromagnetic fields (AC), and electrostatic charges (DC)

Two contributing factors to the increase of indoor air pollution are the growing numbers of chemicals added in household products and the airtight barriers that, while holding down heating and cooling costs, trap these chemicals inside. Before the 1970s energy crisis, the average home's indoor air was exchanged with outdoor air about once every hour. Today's energy-efficient homes' air might be exchanged once every five hours!

A simple solution is to crack open a window in rooms used by the family. Since children spend anywhere from six to ten hours sleeping, be sure that fresh air is pumped in at night. No matter what the weather is outside, be sure that your home is being supplied with fresh air.

Naturally it is best to be aware of what not to bring into a home or what not to use when constructing a home. But that subject is beyond the scope of this book. I suggest you consult what I consider the best book on building healthy homes: *Prescriptions for a Healthy House* by Paula Baker,

Erica Elliot, and John Banta is thorough, written by authors who are respectively an architect, a medical doctor, and an environmental inspector.

Specific Hazards and Toxins

Molds

Molds are known allergens and contributing factors to breathing disorders such as asthma, pneumonia, and immune dysfunction. Children are apt to play on the floor, putting them closer to the source of molds. Molds are also implicated in the mysterious appearance of the deadly Legionnaires' disease and the headaches, general malaise, lethargy, and allergic reactions that are part of the sick building syndrome.

Widely found everywhere in nature, molds, mildew, and fungi, when accumulated in high concentrations, can trigger all sorts of environmental illnesses. Although crawl spaces, basements, and other substructures provide an interior climate where molds and fungi have a field day, there are many other potential areas to examine.

Check for molds anywhere moisture accumulates, including

basements	walls with leaky pipes
bathrooms	carpets
window sills	drains under sinks
laundry rooms	wherever flooding has occurred
ceilings and walls under a	air-conditioning ducts
leaky roof	under vinyl wallpaper

Wiping molds down with bleach (and then carefully wiping the surface dry) after solving the originating problem is one solution. At the end of the book is a resource guide. If you have a severe problem that you cannot handle by yourself, contact an expert.

Flooring

Small children spend a great deal of time crawling, playing, and sleeping on the floor. It is not unusual for young children to play with toys that have touched the floor, to stuff wet fingers in their mouths after roaming the floor's surface, and to burrow their heads in just about any surface around a home. That puts them in direct contact with toxins in flooring.

While **wall-to-wall carpeting** will make a comfortable surface underfoot, it harbors a myriad of potential problems. Synthetic latex-backed carpet emits approximately 100 different gases. If the carpet is glued down, the adhesive most likely will emit formaldehyde gas. Case studies in *Prescriptions for a Healthy House* (Baker, Elliot, and Banta) point out that symptoms such as digestive disorders, frequent episodes of bronchitis, insomnia, chronic coughing, hypoglycemia, lethargy, allergies, and brain fog can be negative reactions to formaldehyde. Also, it is considered a carcinogenic material. Moreover, fibers used to resist dirt and grime typically are coated with chemicals that break down and can be ingested by children who may be putting their fingers inside their mouths while playing on the floor. Older natural fiber carpeting usually doesn't contain fire retardant, and when properly maintained and cleaned is safer as far as air quality is concerned.

Carpet padding may also be releasing all sorts of toxic chemicals in the form of gases, including formaldehyde. Most padding is made of plastic foam or synthetic rubber and contains petroleum products that continue to pollute after installation.

The healthiest flooring is old-fashioned **linoleum**, which is manufactured from linseed oil, cork, and limestone powder with plant- or earth-based

When I laid down wood flooring in my house, I talked to many installers who wouldn't guarantee that the flooring would hold up to heavy traffic unless the wood was coated with a hard polyurethane finish. Whatever the final coating on a product, it will always interface with the environment. A natural wood floor when coated with a clear plastic is in effect a plastic floor and will release gases. I insisted upon a simple wax finish. Yes, I was aware of the necessity of rewaxing the floor often to maintain appearance and protection. The potential inconvenience seemed minor compared with a child's possibly negative reaction to the use of a plastic coating.

color. For comfort you may add area rugs made from natural materials such as cotton, linen, or wool. So long as the fibers have not been coated with chemicals, these materials are not likely to cause any negative reactions.

Plastic and Synthetic Toys

Stuffed toys can be bad news because the materials used to stuff them, such as plastic foam, and the synthetic fabric covers may be loaded with hazardous substances. They also hold static electricity, similar to the way nylon and acrylic carpets do. Whenever you can, buy toys made of natural fibers. But if your child's favorite toy is made of synthetics, cover it with a noncoated all-cotton or linen material.

Toys that children are likely to put in their mouths are a concern. Keep in mind that children under two are likely to put just about anything in their mouths. For this reason, teething toys and other early childhood playthings carry more risk than the toys that older children play with. My advice is to buy natural products for children under two, and older, especially if your child suffers from conditions potentially caused by unsafe environmental conditions, like chronic colds, breathing difficulties, asthma or bronchial conditions, headaches, chronic sinus congestion, hoarseness, and lethargy. Also, curtail purchasing plastic toys, especially if they are colored PVC toys.

AC Electric and DC Magnetic Fields

There is a wide variety of views about the effects of AC electric and DC magnetic fields on the human body. When the book *The Body Electric* was published its message was considered extreme. It argued that because our bodies are electrical systems, other larger electrical fields can interrupt our natural electrical fields, potentially harming our health. When it comes to protecting children whose vulnerable, maturing bodies are like sponges, ready to soak up their environment, it is my opinion that we should err on the side of caution. See the following table for a few facts about the differences between these two potential sources of hazard in order to know what to look for.

Lamps that are not grounded and are positioned less than four feet from a child in bed will produce a negative environmental condition. If an electrical appliance, including a television, stereo, or computer, is in an adjoin-

The Difference Between AC Electric and DC Magnetic Fields

AC ELECTRIC FIELD

Generally flows in a straight line from
point of higher voltage to lower
voltage (usually the earth)

Can be shielded

Present at source even when switches
are turned off

DC MAGNETIC FIELD

Radiates in all directions from a single
source

Difficult but not impossible to shield

Only emits radiation when appliances are
turned on or electrons are moving, as in
a power line

ing room yet sharing the same wall with a child's bed, the DC magnetic fields will pass through the wall into the child's room. DC magnetic fields travel not only through walls but also through floors and ceilings.

The following is a list of common sources of both electric and magnetic fields in a home:

baby monitor
lamps
television
stereo system
kitchen appliances, especially microwave oven
computer
radio alarm clock

cell phone
transformers in fluorescent lights or other products

The longest uninterrupted period of time a child is in one place is in the bedroom. Therefore placing the bed out of harm's way is an important consideration. Only an expert with proper equipment can determine exactly how far away a child must be from electrical and magnetic sources. However, a reasonable way to begin is by positioning the bed as far away as possible from any appliances in the bedroom and placing lamps or other electrical equipment on the other side of the walls of the bedroom at least four feet away. As with all environmental hazards, be particularly alert to any recurring physical or even emotional problems where electromagnetism may be the culprit.

Textiles

What a parent can do about toxins in textiles is to use vigilance and purchase only those products that are nontoxic. Here are a few guidelines.

- Sheets, blankets, pillows, crib bumper pads, and comforters should be made of soft, natural fibers that breathe and absorb. In fact, keep this concept in mind when purchasing anything that comes in contact with a child's skin for any length of time, clothing being the obvious concern.
- Choose natural fibers that are 100 percent organic cotton, linen, and untreated wool.
- Avoid permanent press or other finishes that may improve appearance and eliminate the need for ironing, along with chemicals that retard flammability. The coatings contain formaldehyde or plastic resins that are not always removed by washing.
- Purchase an organic cotton pillowcase when your child is ready for a pillow, typically around the age of twelve months.

Household Products

Dioxin, a by-product of chlorinated compounds, is formed when **chlorine** is used to bleach brown wood pulp white. The bleached pulp is then converted into countless paper products including diapers. It is practically impossible to manufacture a 100 percent environmentally safe product. Although the jury is still out in the United States in regard to whether bleached cloth and paper products affect a child's health, it can't hurt to limit their direct contact with skin. In fact, the Swedish government allows only baby products that are unbleached and chlorine free to be sold there.

The foundation of your child's lifetime health is built during his or her formative years. Take no chances and lean toward caution.

18

Homes Speak

A home speaks a language. Like every other language the words have a meaning but it is the aggregate that constitutes the thought. This book translates the symbols in a home and teaches you how to make your home speak the messages that are best suited for your child. As with all conversations, a home must have a variety of communications. If you tire of hearing a message repeated over and over, then modify your home's message over time.

Adults typically live in fairly static environments, but children don't. Parents may have to focus on making alterations in a home as children grow up. Otherwise, children are more than likely to make changes to suit their needs without parental consent.

Greater importance should be given to elements that are normally thought of as backgrounds like flooring, ceiling, and walls. Children spend a great deal of time gazing at ceilings, which are usually underdecorated. No part of a room should be ignored. Crevices, backs of furnishings, and odd spaces are the stuff that feeds childhood's cravings for diversity. While children need a degree of predictability in the home environment, the rearrangment of toys and furnishings is not a problem for them.

Not only do children move through different stages quickly, but they also respond with more intensity to all sensory stimulus than adults do. I remember my father telling me to enjoy the taste of food because the longer you live the less sensitive you become to taste. Just as our fingers become

I can remember the underside of my family's dining room table with more clarity than its surface. What I loved about the dark, cool spot under the table was a feeling of being protected and safe, free from the attention of adults, yet surrounded by them. It was intriguing to hear conversation from this protected space, far more so than if I was expected to respond. The shapes of shoes, legs, and clothing hidden under the table fascinated me. This childhood experience brings to light that most anything can fascinate a child if he or she is given the chance to explore it unencumbered by expectations. Therefore, we all have in our homes the stuff to beguile our offspring.

callused by use, so do many of the deeply potent senses through which we experience the world. Licking the cookie dough bowl, smelling a fresh flower, or playing with colorful yarns can delight children far more than we adults can imagine. Everyday objects that may bore adults can fascinate children for they constantly construct, shape, and fashion with whatever is available.

Children are our miracles, and they deserve a home that supports interdependence, independence, safety, security, freedom, choice, beauty, comfort, joy, adventure, tranquillity, and patience. That's no small task for us parents! But using a tool like feng shui will increase your assuredness that you are providing a climate that will support your child.

A child's landscape should provide a connection to the past as well as a door that will lead to the future. A parent must balance respect for past accomplishments by promoting a sense of attachment to them as well as a sense of pride in the present. The gold star your child brought home from kindergarten should have its own place yet not upstage the shaky-lined first drawing. A home should reflect the past and present. But most important, it should provide challenges to spark future goals. For example, the books in your home may spark your child's desire to read even before she is old enough to unravel the printed word. What do you have in your home that your child longs to do? Is it a puzzle yet unsolved, a two-wheeler waiting to be mastered, or a game for which skills are yet to be developed? As an adult what is it you still desire to do? Can you imagine a life without goals?

Children live in a context of meaning, and the roles they play form their identities. A personal sense of worth is shaped through interactions. It is through action and doing that children learn to walk a path to learning. The more they are embraced by their environment, the more texture, profusion, and depth it provides, the broader their range of potential enrichment.

An environment is not embellished by what the commercial market produces to entertain children, but by a generous amount of experiences. Shaping a space where your child can flourish is not dependent on the amount of money you spend on equipment and toys, but rather on the amount of time you invest in assuring that there is diversity in options and specificity for your child's individual characteristics. There is no one perfect environment in which all children thrive. There are concepts that when blended into a home can be the springboard for a child's unfolding. If you have the will to understand what is needed and take the time to shape it, then you have what it takes to grow an environment in which all your child's dreams can become reality.

Afterword

Never lose sight of the universal necessity of authenticity.

> *There was a child went forth every day,*
> *And the first object he looked upon, that object he became,*
> *And that object became part of him for the day or a certain part of*
>   *the day,*
> *Or for many years or stretching cycles of years.*

—WALT WHITMAN, *LEAVES OF GRASS*, PUBLISHED IN 1855

Filling a child's interior spaces with things that reflect and are responsive to his or her genuineness will increase that child's potential to express his or her true nature. What more can a parent want than to provide the environment in which children can explore and unravel the mysteries of their potential?

The most important work of my life has been my contribution to the lives of the children with whom I have been blessed: Zachary, Chloe, Barnaby, Shanna, Patrick, Chad, Rebecca, Tommy, Lee, Leni, and soon, baby Kroll.

Bibliography

Ackerman, Diane. *Deep Play*. New York: Random House, 1999.

Ackerman, Diane. *A Natural History of the Senses*, New York: Vintage Books, 1990.

Americans with Disabilities Act. "Checklist for Readily Achievable Barrier Removal," May 16, 1995.

Baker, Paula, Ellion, Erica, and Banta, John. *Prescriptions for a Healthy House*. Santa Fe, NM: InWord Press, 1997.

Birren, Faber. *The Power of Color*. Secaucus, NJ: Citadel Press, 1997.

Campbell, Don. *The Mozart Effect*. New York: Avon Books, 1997.

Center for Accessible Housing. *Recommendations for Accessibility Standards for Children's Environments*. Raleigh, NC: North Carolina State University, January 1992.

Cobb, Edith. *The Ecology of Imagination in Childhood*. Dallas: Spring Publications, 1993.

Davis, Adelle. *Let's Have Healthy Children*. New York: Harcourt, Brace, Jovanovich, 1999.

Fraiberg, Selma. *The Magic Years*. New York: Simon & Schuster, 1996.

Gallagher, Winifed. *Just the Way You Are*. New York: Random House, 1996.

Green, Nancy Sokol. *Poisoning Our Children: Surviving in a Toxic World*. Chicago: Noble Press, 1991.

Hall, Edward T. *The Hidden Dimension*. New York: Doubleday, 1966, 1982.

Jaffke, Freya. *Work and Play in Early Childhood*. Hudson, NY: Anthroposophic Press, 1991.

Maslow, Abraham. *The Farther Reaches of Human Nature*. New York: Arkana Publishers, 1993.

Maslow, Abraham. *Motivation and Personality, Toward a Psychology of Being*, 2nd edition. New York: Harper & Row, 1987.

Mojay, Gabriel. *Aromatherapy for Healing the Spirit*. New York: Gaia Books, 1996.

Nabhan, Gary Paul, and Trimble, Stephen. *The Geography of Childhood*. Boston: Beacon Press, 1994.

Olds, Anita Rui, and Silverstein, Murray. "The Architecture of Day Care and Health Care Environments." Boston: Child Care Design Institute, Harvard University, June 1999.

Thomas, Marlo. *Free to Be You and Me*. Performed by Marlo Thomas and 1972 television cast. BMG/Arista, 1972.

Whitman, Walt. *Leaves of Grass*. New York: Doubleday, 1940.

Wydra, Nancilee. *Designing Your Happiness*. Torrence, CA: Heian Publishers, 1995.

Wydra, Nancilee. *Feng Shui: The Book of Cures*. Lincolnwood, IL: NTC/Contemporary, 1996.

Wydra, Nancilee. *Feng Shui and How to Look Before You Love*. Lincolnwood, IL: NTC/Contemporary, 1998.

Wydra, Nancilee. *Feng Shui Goes to the Office*. Lincolnwood, IL: NTC/Contemporary, 2000.

Wydra, Nancilee. *Feng Shui in the Garden*. Lincolnwood, IL: NTC/Contemporary, 1997.

Resources

Feng Shui Institute of America (FSIA)
P.O. Box 488, Wabasso, FL 32970
Phone: (888) 488-FSIA (3742)
Fax: (561) 589-1611
E-mail: Windwater8@aol.com
Websites: www.windwater.com (for information about feng shui
    professional education and list of consultants worldwide)
www.efengshuiusa.com (for *free* feng shui information)

Feng Shui Institute International (FSII)
7547 Bruns Court, Canal Winchester, OH 43110
Phone: (614) 837-8370
Fax: (614) 834-9760
E-mail: fengshuimasters1@aol.com
Membership organization for feng shui professionals trained by FSIA

Full Circle Architects
Lenore Baigelman
1624 Northland Avenue, Highland Park, IL 60035
Phone: (847) 831-0884
Fax: (847) 831-0286
E-mail: lenorewb@aol.com

Healthy Habitats
Tara Andrea Swierkosz
2367 Ruta Corta, Santa Fe, NM 87505
Phone: (505) 438-7793
Fax: (505) 438-8747
E-mail: maboudtara@compuserve.com

Healthy Homes
Carol Venolia
P.O. Box 4417, Santa Rosa, CA 95402-4417
Phone: (707) 579-2201
E-mail: CVenolia@compuserve.com

Image Diagnostics
Beverly Payeff
P.O. Box 136, Brookline, NH 03033
Phone: (800) 303-0056
Fax: (603) 672-2848
E-mail: imagedi@tiac.net

International Institute for Bau-Biologie & Ecology
Helmut Ziehe
1401 A Cleveland Street, Clearwater, FL 33755
Phone: (727) 461-4371
Fax: (727) 441-4373
E-mail: baubiologie@earthlink.net
Website: www.bau-biologieusa.com

Soul Essentials
P.O. Box 488, Wabasso, FL 32970
Phone: (888) 780-SOUL (7685)
Fax: (561) 589-1611
E-mail: Cures4U@aol.com
Charts, wheels, and other supports for utilizing feng shui

Angel Thompson
Astrology/Feng Shui
1809 Washington Way, Venice, CA 90291
Phone: (310) 821-2527
Fax: (310) 822-9846
E-mail: FengShuiLA@aol.com

Index